Teachers' Guide

HOPSCOTCH EDUCATIONAL PUBLISHING

Non-fiction writing

SCAFFOLDS

Written by
Eileen Jones

Published by
Hopscotch Educational Publishing Ltd
Unit 2
The Old Brushworks
56 Pickwick Road
Corsham
Wiltshire
SN13 9BX

01249 701701

© 2003 Hopscotch Educational Publishing

Written by Eileen Jones
Series design by Blade Communications
Cover illustration by Kirsty Wilson
Illustrated by Susan Hutchison
Printed by Athenaeum Press Ltd, Gateshead

ISBN 1-904307-06-X

Eileen Jones hereby asserts her moral right to be
identified as the author of this work in accordance
with the Copyright, Designs and Patents Act, 1988.

Non-fiction writing
SCAFFOLDS

CONTENTS

Non-fiction writing scaffolds for Year 4

INTRODUCTION

Non-fiction Writing Scaffolds for Year 4 is intended for use in schools to help teach children how to write effectively in a variety of non-fiction genres. It improves children's ability to organise their writing so that it has purpose by familiarising them with a system of planning which they can apply to any title. As they work through the units, the children assemble a portfolio of non-fiction texts containing genre-specific vocabulary and writing features. The chosen text types correspond with those in the Literacy Framework's text-level objectives.

Many non-fiction texts are essentially cross-curricular. Thus the ability to write specifically and purposefully about a subject will benefit other areas of study.

Each unit includes information and activities on at least one sentence-level objective. Therefore the book also enhances the children's knowledge of grammar, punctuation and style.

THE PROGRAMME CONTAINS:

a teachers' book comprising:

■ notes for teachers on the genres
■ a bibliography for each genre
■ copies of exemplar texts with teaching notes
■ guidance on how to develop grammar and punctuation skills in children's writing
■ guidance on how to write in the particular genre and on specific features of each non-fiction text.

a resource book of photocopiable material comprising:

■ illustrated versions of the exemplar texts especially produced for children
■ notes for the children on understanding the grammar and punctuation (optional reference material)
■ photocopiable activity sheets to reinforce the grammar and punctuation (optional)
■ notes and tips for the children on writing non-fiction texts (optional reference material)
■ differentiated scaffolds which give the children choices and guide them through the course of the text they are about to write
■ vocabulary banks for them to use and add to.

HOW TO USE THE PROGRAMME

1 After examining texts in the target genre, read and discuss the exemplar text with the children, using the notes in the margin to highlight the examples of the unit's teaching point and writing feature. The children should follow the text using their own illustrated version from the resource book.

2 Next, read through and explain the 'Understanding the grammar and punctuation' section of the unit. The children can do the activities together, either orally or using whiteboards, or independently on paper.

3 Then explain the 'Helpful hints' and 'Writing features' sections of the unit to the children.

4 Read through the scaffolds with the children. Then give them the differentiated word banks and ask them to record their own vocabulary suggestions in the space provided.

5 Give the children time to plan, write and edit their non-fiction text. Each child can then store the best copies in a writing folder.

NOTES

When using the scaffolds, give the children strict time limits to plan and write each of the sections. This will give them practice in writing timed non-fiction texts as preparation for the Key Stage 2 writing test.

However, the system is entirely flexible. The activities in each unit, from reading the exemplar to composing their own text using the scaffolds, can be used in shared or guided time, with the children working collaboratively or individually.

The order of activities for each unit corresponds exactly with the sequence for the teaching of writing outlined in Grammar for Writing (DfEE 0107/200). First the model can be discussed and its grammatical and thematic features interrogated during shared reading. Next the grammar and punctuation activities can be undertaken to reinforce the children's understanding of the relevant sentence-level objectives. The helpful hints section, scaffolds, and vocabulary banks support the teacher and children in shared writing sessions and in subsequent guided and independent writing.

The method works well with children of all abilities and with bilingual pupils, as it offers the security of a detailed framework and a bank of appropriate vocabulary together with the challenge of a grammar and writing features component for each unit.

The units fulfil the text-level and sentence-level requirements of the NLS Framework for Year 4 and revise components from Year 3. The following units may be used specifically in literacy lessons or they may be linked with work in other curriculum areas and used accordingly.

TERM 1
UNIT 1
Genre: newspaper report: sports event (T16; T17; T18; T20)
Grammar: verbs and verb tenses (S2);
Punctuation: direct speech (Yr3 revision)
Writing features: headlines, style, verb tense and language (T24)

UNIT 2
Genre: newspaper/magazine article: holiday travel (T16; T17; T19; T20; T21)
Grammar: powerful verbs; adverbs (S3)
Punctuation: commas (revision: lists, direct speech)
Writing features: headlines, presentation, content, language and layout (T24)

UNIT 3
Genre: instructions: how to make a mobile of flying owls (T22)
Grammar: imperative verbs (S4)
Punctuation: organisational devices, such as numbered and bulleted lists (T22)
Writing features: layout, chronological order, the use of labelled diagrams (T25; T26)

TERM 2
UNIT 4
Genre: report: notes and final text on Henry VIII (T15)
Grammar: adjectives: comparative and superlative (S1)
Punctuation: apostrophes: singular and plural possession (S2)
Writing features: orientation, chronology, time connectives (T21; T22)

UNIT 5
Genre: explanation text: electricity (T20)
Grammar: verb tense (revision: Term 1)
Punctuation: subheadings, organisational devices, such as numbered and bulleted lists
Writing features: opening statements, logical and chronological order, technical information, diagrams (T24; T25)

UNIT 6
Genre: explanation text: making glass bottles (T20)
Grammar: paragraphs and link phrases
Punctuation: connectives (S4)
Writing features: opening statements, presentation, sequential order, sequential connectives, tone (T24; T25)

TERM 3
UNIT 7
Genre: advertisements (T18; T19)
Grammar: different types of adjectives (revision: Term 2)
Punctuation: exclamation marks, dashes, colons, bullet points (S2)
Writing features: layout, symbols, speech bubbles, illustrations (T25)

UNIT 8
Genre: discussion text: letters to the press about school uniform (T16)
Grammar: connectives (S4)
Punctuation: setting out formal letters
Writing features: presentation of point of view, language used (T23)

UNIT 9
Genre: editoria: tabloid and broadsheet presentation of viewpoint on a traffic issue (T16; T17; T18)
Grammar: connectives (S4)
Punctuation: the use of inverted commas when quoting
Writing features: presentation, verb tense, style, emotive language (T23)

Newspaper reports

A newspaper or magazine article is written for interest; a report is written to convey news. This distinction between articles and reports is important. This exemplar text is a report and the topic is sport.

The sports reporter wants the reader to read his article. He is giving information that he hopes the reader is going to find important: the reader needs to know if his team (or sportsperson) has won! The main facts must be conveyed quickly and clearly, and in crisp language appropriate to the sport. Descriptions of the action tend to use familiar similes and metaphors, sometimes rather worn out, but still enjoyed in the sporting world; for example, 'He ran straight as an arrow.' Sports readers enjoy the language they know from television punditry but there is certainly room for some sparkling originality.

After that, much depends on the space the editor allows. Further details about the event and individual competitors add interest, as do tantalising hints of possible behind-the-scenes action, perhaps offering hints of change/upset/disharmony/intrigue. Note the difference between hints and statements, and ensure that the children recognise this distinction between fact and opinion. The paper cannot afford to lay itself open to legal action!

Further interest is often provided by more detailed reference to one individual, perhaps in the form of quoted words. The paper may have secured an interview, or have access to the opinion of a known expert, such as a famous, former player. All this could offer a different slant.

The writer must keep the reader's attention right to the last word, so a good finish is important. Information about the future, or questions which will only be answered by the next match, are good devices.

Reports have typical features:
- a headline – to catch the reader's eye and to encourage them to read the story;
- a subheading – adds information to the headline. It does not have to be a sentence.
- a topic sentence – usually the first sentence of the report to explain what the story is about;
- short paragraphs – to enable the reader to locate information quickly;
- columns – to make the article easier to read;
- use of different type-faces – to add interest and enhance the design;
- photographs – to add interest and authenticity to the story;
- quotations – to give an air of truth or reality to the story.

Journalistic writing

Examples of journalistic writing

Newspapers – local, regional, national; tabloids and broadsheets.

Greek Gazette by F Fleming('Newspaper History' series, Usborne, 1997)

The Roman News by Philip Gates and Ghislaine Lawrence (Walker Books, 1994) Others in the series cover Egyptians, Aztecs, Vikings, Greeks and the Stone Age.

1910s by Margaret Sharman ('Take Ten Years' series, Evans Brothers, 1991) Uses newspaper reports from the period.

Good Writing by William Edmonds and Karen Wilbraham ('Guides to Good English' series, Kingfisher, 1989) Includes a section on reporting.

The children's illustrated version of the report is on page 6 of the resource book.

A *newspaper report*

JP LIFTS THE CUP![1]

How did they do it? Read on![2]

By Matt Jones[3]

Last Saturday, in biting, blustery[4] conditions, on freshly-marked netball courts, the annual local tournament was won by John Parsons School, with an astounding total of 96 points. The school now reigns as this season's area champion.[5]

[6]This title – Worthshire Champions – is always a prized one, and must have brought special pleasure after the school's catastrophic sporting year. Their newly-appointed young, female,[7] sports teacher, Miss Crumble, has been experiencing obvious difficulties:[8] joint last in the under-11 football tournament in April;[9] half a team left trampled underfoot[10] at most of the winter's cross-country meetings;[9] the worst ever[11] display of catching at July's rounders tournament;[9] a cricket team that clearly relished the taste of duck;[12] and then there was netball. Those scores haven't been worth adding up!

However, all this changed on Saturday when the netball team beat all comers. Girls who didn't seem to be able to see the net all season[11] were suddenly firing balls home with pinpoint

The John Parsons School team hold up the Worthshire Champions cup

accuracy;[13] passing was fast and flowing; footwork[4] was sure; and teamwork was brilliant. What had happened?[14]

"Miss Crumble was employed as a sports teacher!" boomed[15] Mr Rankle, the headmaster, to the local press. "She knew what was expected of her. My governors and I value sport. I simply explained[16] to Miss Crumble the importance of today. The hosts never come last, and I didn't want to become the butt of the other heads' jokes."

For her part, Emma Crumble looked exhausted. "It's mainly relief I feel," she said. "I've been at school all hours coaching these girls. If they'd lost today, I dread to think what I'd have lost!"[17]

1 Headline grabs attention by its content and its bold, visual style. It is short enough for the reader to take in at a glance, and the exclamation mark hints at surprise and excitement to follow.

2 Sub head slightly smaller. It tempts the reader to read on; the use of an unanswered question helps.

3 Inclusion of the writer's name is usual at this point.

4 Alliteration – effective use of the same sound at the beginning of words.

5 The first paragraph contains the main facts about the event.

6 The writer moves to more detail about the event.

7 Such detailed information as this would have to be left out if there was a shortage of column space.

8 Colon used to introduce a list.

9 Semi colons used to separate items in list.

10 Hyperbole (light-hearted exaggeration).

11 Probably an exaggeration, but conveys the desired message.

12 Original and effective use of imagery. (Makes the connection between eating duck and scoring nought – a duck.)

13 An effective phrase.

14 An effective use of a question: the reader will want to discover the answer.

15 A strong verb (as opposed to just using 'said').

16 Is there a veiled threat to Miss Crumble's future employment contained in these two words?

17 A good example of implicit meaning – the reader understands that the dread is of losing her job, even though the writer does not state it.

Understanding the grammar and punctuation

Grammar pointers

Verbs

The verb is the essential word in every sentence. Defined simply, a verb is a doing or being word, but by this stage it is important to point out that more than one word may make up the verb. For example:

> *What had happened?*

'Happened' is clearly the main action word or verb. Nevertheless, 'had' is part of the verb; it is called the auxiliary verb. The text contains numerous examples for the children to identify:

> *have brought*
>
> *'ve been* (short for 'have been')
>
> *'d lost* (had lost)

These auxiliary verbs have been used to put the principal verb into the correct tense; in a report, the past tense is generally used.

Verb tenses

'Tense' means 'time'. Hence, verb tenses place the action in a timeframe. Essentially, there are three tenses: past, present and future. The mental addition of yesterday, today and tomorrow could be useful aids to the children's correct identification of tense. In a report such as the exemplar text, the past tense is usually used.

Punctuation pointers

Direct speech

This means writing down the actual words spoken. Only those precise spoken words are placed inside the quotation marks. Any sentence containing direct speech is subject to numerous rules of punctuation.

- ✦ If part of the sentence is spoken, and part of it not, the two parts must be separated, usually by a comma. For example:

  > *"It's mainly relief I feel," she said.*
  >
  > *One woman moaned, "My child won't be coming here again."*

- ✦ This comma may be replaced by a question mark or an exclamation mark. For example:

  > *"Miss Rankle is supposed to be a sports teacher!" shouted Mr Rankle.*
  >
  > *"Where's the rest of my team?" she asked nervously.*

- ✦ The first spoken word in a sentence always begins with a capital letter. For example:

  > *Looking furious, one of the parents asked, "May I have a word?"*
  >
  > *An onlooker shouted, "Well done!"*

- ✦ But be careful if the direct speech in a sentence is split up. For example:

  > *"Miss Crumble came as a sports teacher," boomed Mr Rankle, "and I knew she'd get there in the end."*

  and does not require a capital letter because it is not the first word Mr Rankle said in the sentence.

- ✦ Finally, a new paragraph is begun whenever someone begins/finishes speaking. (Obviously, you don't begin the paragraph in the middle of a sentence.) For example:

  > *Many of the spectators were looking fed up, and a few looked distinctly angry. Emma was praying that her team would at least do a little better than last time.*
  >
  > *"What exactly do you teach them in the netball lesson?" came a sharp voice.*
  >
  > *Emma turned her head to see a large, fear-inducing woman standing next to her. She gulped and tried to think of something to say.*
  >
  > *"I just do my best," was the feeble reply.*
  >
  > *"Well it obviously isn't good enough!"**
  >
  > *"I would like to do better."**
  >
  > *At that moment, a roar interrupted the tense conversation: John Parsons had actually scored! Emma's prayers had been answered.*

* The writer has no need to say who is speaking; starting a new paragraph makes it clear.

Note that writers adhere to these strict rules to a greater or lesser degree, so be prepared for exceptions when the children look for examples in books.

> The children's version of these notes is on page 7 of the resource book.

The writing features of newspaper reports

Headlines

These obviously carry great importance and, when thinking about their composition, the writer should focus on:

✦ the need to attract attention;

✦ the selection of key words rather than lengthy sentences;

✦ the devices used to draw the reader into the article;

✦ details such as

1. the choice of construction; for example a question or a statement:

   – *How did they do it?*

   – *They did it.*

2. the choice of punctuation; such as the use of an exclamation mark instead of a full stop.

Style

Level of formality

Sport is an area in which most readers feel knowledgeable and on which they have their own definite views. They want to be treated as equals, feeling involved in the report, and not overawed by it. This means the tone should be exciting and fast-moving, never boring or over-technical. In the exemplar text we can feel that we are listening to Emma Crumble as she is interviewed. When the reporter writes 'What had happened?' at the end of the third paragraph in the exemplar report, he hopes that is exactly what the reader is thinking.

Tense

A report, whether sports or news, should generally be written in the past tense.

> *the annual local tournament was won by John Parsons School*

> *that clearly relished*

> *Emma Crumble looked exhausted.*

Language

Vivid

Sports reporting tends towards the extreme. Here, strong adjectives are abundant.

> *'prized', 'catastrophic', 'exhausted', 'astounding', 'biting', 'blustery', 'pinpoint'*

The impact of a report may be enhanced by putting adjectives beginning with the same sound in close proximity – alliteration.

> *biting, blustery conditions*

> *fast and flowing*

Hyperbole is a form of exaggeration that is not meant to be taken too seriously. It is a device whereby exaggeration creates the desired effect. Were the pupils really 'left trampled underfoot'? It's more likely that one or other just slipped. Was it 'the worst ever display of catching'? Probably not, but the words create a good visual image of an extremely poor team of fielders. 'Pinpoint' accuracy almost certainly overstates the girls' skill, but it emphasises their improvement.

Some individual words also overstate the facts, for example 'catastrophic', 'astounding' and 'brilliant', but the effect is good, the meaning clear and the language is what we expect. Ask the children to consider the literal meanings of these words. Is the reporter probably exaggerating? Which could be literally true? Such language is common in sports reporting, but can be over employed. Talk to the children about striking a balance between using language appropriate to that sport; for example:

> *He smashed home another of his great winners.*

> *She shot with deadly accuracy.*

and the clichés that have been used so often we all see them as a joke; for example:

> *Well, that football match was really a game of two halves.*

A certain amount of originality will make a report stand out; the image of eating duck is effective hyperbole because it probably has to be thought about for a moment before its meaning is clear.

> *a cricket team that enjoyed the taste of duck*

> There are helpful hints for children on writing a newspaper report on page 10 of the resource book.

Newspaper and magazine articles

Articles may be on all manner of subjects, but are likely to feature in a specialist magazine or a dedicated section of a newspaper. The focus of an article is interest, thereby differing from a report, where the focus is news. In a news report, facts should be adhered to, with little intrusion by the writer; in an article, there is ample room and desire for the writer's personal opinion. Use of the first person is, therefore, prevalent in this genre.

As with all journalistic writing, attracting and retaining the attention of the audience are of paramount importance. Initially, a headline attracts the attention; after that, the article must keep the readers interested. The writer will often begin with a broad introductory sentence about the topic, informing readers what the article is about, before moving to greater detail.

Subheadings can help to divide the text into manageable sections, and a timely use of paragraphs avoids the audience losing interest. The writer where relevant will also use pictures – illustrations, diagrams or photographs – which give further appeal or information for the audience. Where relevant, captions are used to explain the pictures.

In addition, the writing must be vivid and stimulating. The choice of language is important, with strong impact needed, with powerful verbs and informative adverbs clearly helpful. Readers will be keen to detect the writer's views. However, the writer must be well-informed on the chosen topic, if those views are to be taken seriously. Unless there are supporting facts and details, the article will lack credibility and also interest.

Newspaper and magazine articles

Examples of journalistic articles

Make a collection of newspapers of different types – local, regional, national; broadsheet, tabloid – for the children to examine.

Create Your Own Magazine by Barbara Taylor (Simon and Schuster Young Books, 1993)

The Roman News by Philip Gates and Ghislaine Lawrence ('Historical newspapers' series, Walker Books, 1994) Also in the series *The Aztec News*, *The Viking News* and *The Egyptian News*

Greek Gazette by F Fleming ('Newspaper history' series, Usborne, 1997)

The children's version of the article is on page 17 of the resource book.

A *magazine article*

The World At Our Feet[1]

By Sarah Khan[2]

Yesterday[3]

Holidays are important to people.[4] The grandparents of today recall vividly[5] their summer holidays: they tussled[6] with the guy-ropes of a tent; they cowered[6] inside sleeping bags, as insects attacked[7] and bats squeaked[8]; their shoes squelched disgustingly[9] as they were forced again to trudge between tent and site shop; their faces smarted and their legs screamed[10] pitifully for rest after a long day of scouring windswept towns, in search of shelter and amusement. They were relieved to go home.

People began to explore places further afield, such as France

It cannot always have been so unrelentingly bad. However,[11] it was these memories that initially drove people away from Britain. Greater prosperity, as well as cheaper travel,[12] sliced open the world. People started confidently to criss-cross France and Spain, demanding comfort, and, most of all, to bask luxuriously in warmth. Demands that once were craved[13] had been satisfied.

A scene from a family holiday in the 1950s

Today[3]

In fact,[14] demands multiply. As the price of package holidays has plummeted,[15] so we beg[15] for greater variety. Marching further,[16] we have discovered the charms of Cyprus and Greece;[17] we wrap ourselves cosily in the greater heat of Turkey and Tunisia and we have been lured willingly[18] to more exotic destinations, such as Egypt and Tunisia.

Today people travel the world looking for exotic holidays

However, my adult children now jeer[15] at such commonplace destinations. As the

1 Headline is in large, bold print. It is slightly enigmatic, encouraging us to read on in order to find out more.

2 The writer's name usually appears here.

3 Use of sub-heads helps the reader and keeps his attention.

4 An initial, short, topic sentence informs the reader immediately of the article's main focus.

5 An adverb of manner. There are several used to make this text more effective.

6 Strong verbs are used, giving very graphic images of the children's problems.

7 Good choice of verbs and adverb makes insects seem like spiteful people.

8 An onomatopoeic verb.

9 Effective pairing of verb and adverb; we can almost see, feel and hear the muddy mess.

10 Powerful verb – the legs have feelings of their own, crying out with pain.

11 Comma used after introductory word to separate it from the rest of the sentence.

12 Commas used as a pair, separating a phrase that occurs in the middle of a sentence from the rest of the sentence.

13 Strong verb, emphasising the extent of people's demands.

14 Comma used after a short phrase, separating it from the following main clause. Notice that the main clause is equally short, but is a clause because it contains the verb 'multiply'.

15 Another powerful verb.

16 Adverb of place.

17 Semicolon used to separate places in a list.

18 Effective combination of verb and adverb, as they seem to be contradictory. 'Lured' implies deceit, but 'willingly' says that people wanted to go anyway.

cost of air travel tumbles <u>further, so</u>[19] their world shrinks. One has spent this summer in Australia; another pores <u>intently</u>[20] over her plans for a trip to China; while the third maps an itinerary to enjoy <u>later</u>[21] the sights, beauty and culture of Malaysia. Meanwhile, South America still beckons pleadingly.

<u>Tomorrow</u>[3]

<u>So where will their children roam?</u>[22] <u>How far will their roads lead?</u>[22] <u>I</u>[23] have my own theories here: <u>I</u>[23] believe they will explore and discover Britain. Scoff at that idea if you wish, but at least consider it seriously for a moment. Those children will grow up unaware of so much: cliff walks in <u>Wales;</u>[24] the colours of <u>St.</u>

The joy of cliff walking in Wales is not to be missed

<u>Ives</u>[24] that have inspired artists; the beauty of the <u>Lake District;</u>[24] and the rugged magnificence of <u>Scotland.</u>[24]

The calm pleasure of painting the scene

Then one day, original brochures will burst upon the scene. These will promise unique opportunities for excitement. They will portray places excelling all their childhood memories. <u>And these places? Where will they be? The places will simply be here.</u>[25]

Sarah Khan holds a PhD in Travel and Psychology and has produced many papers on tourism. The author of 'Whither Now?', this year's Farmhouse Award winner, she is currently researching hiking holidays on the Yorkshire Moors.

19 Comma used to separate two clauses linked by a conjunction.

20 Informative adverb of manner, adding to the detail of the text.

21 Adverb of time.

22 Wise use of questions, which the writer will then go on to answer. The reader will want to read the answer.

23 Use of the first person (I). The writer's personal views are quite often given in an article.

24 Place names are important in this article about travel, if the writer's views are to be taken seriously.

25 An effective ending, using a short question and answer technique.

Understanding the grammar and punctuation

Grammar pointers

Powerful verbs

A powerful verb can contribute greatly to the quality of a piece of writing. In addition to fulfilling its grammatical role as the linchpin of the sentence, it adds intensity to the action. For example:

> *original brochures will <u>burst</u> upon the scene*

> *after a long day of <u>scouring</u> windswept town,*

A powerful verb can also save words:

> *their legs <u>screamed</u> pitifully*

'Screamed' supplies implicit information. It does not just tell us that their legs hurt, but suggests the additional idea that the children were probably crying out with pain.

> *they <u>cowered</u> inside sleeping bags*

Here the verb presents a strong visual image of a child curling up, trying to find protection from attacking insects.

> *once were <u>craved</u>*

With one word, 'craved', the writer conveys the strength of people's demands, comparing them to those of a starving person for food.

Adverbs

An adverb describes or modifies a verb, an adjective or another adverb. It is the first of these functions that the children most need to think about in this unit.

Point out that adverbs can be powerful tools in improving the effectiveness and accuracy of much of their writing. They will find it easy to identify many of these words, as they often end in the suffix 'ly'.

> *People started <u>confidently</u> to criss-cross France and Spain , demanding comfort, and, most of all, to bask <u>luxuriously</u> in warmth.*

There are, however, numerous exceptions to the 'ly' convention. For example:

> *Demands that <u>once</u> were craved had been satisfied.*

> *as they were forced <u>again</u>*

Types of adverbs

In many cases, the adverb answers the question 'How?' This is the most common function of the adverb. However, there are other classifications of adverbs.

The categories of adverbs are:

- Manner (How?)

  > *another pores <u>intently</u> over her plans*

  > *still beckons <u>pleadingly</u>*

- Time (When?)

  > *to enjoy <u>later</u>*

- Place (Where?)

  > *The places will simply be <u>here</u>.*

- Degree (How much?)

  > *<u>so</u> unrelentingly bad*

  > *<u>such</u> commonplace destinations*

In the last category, the adverb modifies an adjective or another adverb. Be wary of confusing the children at this stage, as it is the first category that they will probably make most use of.

Punctuation pointers

Using commas to mark grammatical boundaries

A comma separates different grammatical parts of a sentence, marking the boundary between one and the next.

1. It can separate two discrete clauses which are currently joined by a conjunction. For example:

   > *Scoff at that idea if you wish, but at least consider it seriously for a moment.*

2. It can mark the boundary between the main clause and an additional phrase or word. For example:

   > *In fact, demands multiply.*

   > *However, it was these memories that initially drove people away from Britain and enticed them to the sun.*

   (Remember – a clause can form a complete sentence; a phrase is a group of words that do not form a sentence.)

Understanding the grammar and punctuation

3. The commas may work in pairs. This happens when the aside, or extra part, is placed in the middle of the sentence. This is because now there are obviously two boundaries; both must be marked. For example:

> *Greater prosperity, as well as cheaper travel, sliced open the world.*

> *and, most of all, to bask luxuriously in warmth*

Encourage the children to read their own texts to one another. This will help them to identify where commas are needed.

Emphasise the link between the punctuation work in this unit and the general need to edit and revise their own writing.

> The children's version of these notes is on page 19 of the resource book.

The writing features of articles

The aim of an article is to attract and then hold the reader's interest. The first aim is achieved by a bold headline, but the second must be achieved by presentation, content and vivid language. Remind the children of the conventions of newspaper layout.

Structure

Headlines
Focus on the purpose of a newspaper headline, and spend time considering ways to make it effective. For example:
+ the use of questions
+ the choice of punctuation
+ the consideration of vocabulary

Opening sentence
The opening sentence needs to be kept short, and it should immediately inform the audience what the article is going to be about. For example:

> *Holidays are important to people.*

At once, it is clear that the topic for this article is holidays.

Separating text
Discuss the need to present writing in manageable sections, with the aim of sustaining interest.

A paragraph is a distinct section of a text. The writer moves on to a new paragraph when the present one is becoming too long, or a change of content demands the move. Here a line is drawn under the grandparents' memories:

> *They were relieved to go home.*

Again a good closure to a paragraph is achieved here, when the past is finished with:

> *Demands that once were craved had been satisfied.*

When the justification for the separation is not made clear by the end of one paragraph, it can be achieved in the first sentence of the next:

> *However, my adult children now jeer at such commonplace destinations.*

Such changes in people, time, place, or attitudes are clearly good moments to begin a new paragraph. Here time and events change:

> *Then one day, original brochures will burst upon the scene*

Headings and subheadings
These are helpful organisational devices, indicating what a section is to be about. For example, the writer tells the audience she is moving to the future:

> *Tomorrow*

> *So where will their children roam?*

Endings
Stress to the children that interest must be maintained to the very end, so the final sentence matters. Here, for example, the sentence is short, and withholds an important idea until the very end:

> *The places will simply be here.*

Credibility
Talk to the children about the need to show knowledge of a subject when writing an article, as opposed to just interest. An article needs some real facts (for example, names of people, places) to support the writer's opinions. For example, real facts and place names are used here, proving that the writer knows what she is talking about:

> *Those children will grow up unaware of so much: <u>cliff walks in Wales</u>; <u>the colours of St. Ives that have inspired artists</u>; the <u>beauty of the Lake District</u>; and the rugged <u>magnificence of Scotland</u>.*

Similarly, in the 'Today' section of the article, the choice of places is sufficiently exotic to both provoke interest and make clear the writer's knowledge of modern thinking:

> *One has spent this summer in <u>Australia</u>; another pores intently over her plans for a trip to <u>China</u>; while the third maps an itinerary to enjoy later the sights, beauty and culture of <u>Malaysia</u>. Meanwhile, <u>South America</u> still beckons pleadingly.*

Person
A significant part of an article will probably be in the third person (he, she, they, it), but articles are also vehicles for personal views: the first person (I) will, therefore, be used. For example:

> *<u>I</u> have my own theories here: <u>I</u> believe they will explore and discover Britain.*

A statement of personal opinion is a proper feature of articles, and the children should be encouraged to include it in their writing.

The writing features of articles

Language

Personal involvement

The writer of an article is likely to have an interest in his topic, and the language used reflects this. It may reveal an involvement and an attitude to the topic written about.

In the following example it is clear that the writer holds strong feelings about the British countryside, and the feelings are positive ones. A single word can make that obvious:

> the colours of St. Ives that have <u>inspired</u> artists; the <u>beauty</u> of the Lake District; and the rugged <u>magnificence</u> of Scotland

Vocabulary

The previous point shows the impact a single word may have, so talk to the children about variety in words and using them with precision. Adjectives, strong verbs and adverbs need to be selected with care, with the latter two, in particular, able to offer impact to an article.

There are helpful hints for children on writing an article on page 22 of the resource book.

Instructions

The purpose of this text type is to give instructions on how something should be made or done. It differs from many other texts as it does not work to hold its readers' interest: it is there to direct. It is an informative text, but one that has an outcome. This outcome needs to be made clear at the outset, and it is the title that fulfils this role.

The pattern for the whole text is established immediately, with information set out clearly and superfluous language pruned. Illustrations and diagrams may be needed, and organisational devices such as subheadings and numbered lists are valuable, identifying the need for chronological steps. The message needs to be clear: a sequence must be adhered to.

This chronology is apparent in the language as well as the layout. Written instructions make frequent use of time connectives, there not just to hold the text together, but also to emphasise the importance of keeping to an order.

Imperative or present tense verbs are used and the reader is rarely addressed directly. Command sentences issue directions for achieving the goal.

The successful instruction writer needs:

✦ to define his audience and the purpose of his instructions;

✦ to be aware of how much the reader will already know about the situation and the process before he begins so that he can target his instructions according to his audience;

✦ to have a thorough understanding of the procedure, to be able to visualise it in detail, and to try to capture that awareness on paper;

✦ to put himself in the place of the person who is trying to use the instructions;

✦ to check that his instructions follow a logical sequence and are unambiguous;

✦ to keep terminology to a minimum and fully explain unfamiliar terms;

✦ to use diagrams and illustrations when explaining how to make or assemble items, and these need to be straightforward, clearly labelled and easy to refer to.

Instructions

Examples of instructions

✦ Instructions for using a mobile phone, a personal stereo and hi-fi equipment.
✦ Assembly instructions for toys, furniture and gadgets.
✦ Cookery recipes.
✦ Art, craft and technology books.
✦ Rules for board-games.
✦ Instructions on how to look after machines.

The Usborne Book of Pop-ups by Richard Dungworth and Ray Gibson (Usborne, 1997)

I Can Make Presents by Rachel Wright ('Look and Make' series, Watts, 1997)

Buildings by Pam Beasant ('How to Draw' series, Usborne, 1991)

Paper folding by Clive Stevens ('Step-by-step' series, Heinemann Library, 2001)

The children's version of the instructions is on page 29 of the resource book.

How to make a Hogwarts' owl mobile[1]

You've read the book, seen the film, and even bought the odd card.

What else can you do?

Of course! Create your own Hogwarts' dormitory.

What you need[2]

- [3] Card
- Paint
- A hole punch
- Strong thread (nylon thread will not break)
- Straws (preferably firm, plastic ones)
- Glue
- Coloured sticky paper/fluorescent pens
- Tracing paper

What to do[4]

1. Cut pieces of card of the same size. About 15 by 20cm is a good size to work with.

2. On rough paper of the same size, practise drawing an owl, perhaps trying two or three different views. (It is worth spending time on this part to create lifelike birds.)

3. Decide which of the owls you are going to use: one, two or three types.

4. Place tracing paper on top of an owl, and go over your drawing in pencil.

5. Now place the tracing paper on the card, and go over those lines again, pressing firmly.

6. Remove the tracing paper, and you should be able to see your owl on the card. If the drawing isn't clear, repeat instruction 5.

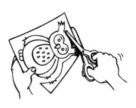

7. Next,[5] cut out the owl.

8. Work out how many and which type of owls you want. (A total of ten would be effective.)

9. Repeat[6] instructions 4, 5, 6 and 7 until you have all your owls.

10. Paint[6] the owls and leave them to dry.

11. Finally,[5] add any extra features you think are needed: for example, eyes, beak and talons, using sticky paper/fluorescent pens/paint.

---

1 The intended outcome is stated at the start.

2 Use is made of the organisational device of a subheading. Four subheadings are used in the text to separate sections of information. It is a good aid to clarity.

3 Bullet points are another effective organisational device. They make it easier to read the information quickly. As they are used on different lines, they reinforce the separation of one item from another.

4 A numbered list is another way to organise information. It also gives a clear sequence to the instructions.

5 A time connective. The sequential steps are emphasised by these link words. They give cohesion, as well as a time order, to the instructions.

6 'Repeat' and 'Paint' are both examples of the imperative form of the verb. This language of command is in constant use throughout the text.

How to assemble your owl mobile

a)[7] First,[5] punch a hole in each owl. The place will depend on how you want that owl to hang.

b) Next,[5], cut a small groove (not all the way through) about 1cm from each end of every straw.

c) Fasten some thread securely[8] through the hole in an owl and tie it beside the groove on a straw, so that the owl dangles.

9

d) Repeat[10] instruction c) for every owl. (Give[10] yourself plenty of space to place the finished straws out of the way.)

e) Now[5] you are going to start building your mobile from the bottom upwards. Each straw (complete with owl) must hang level from the straw above.

f) Take[10] the first straw. Find and mark the point where you need to hold the straw so that it hangs level.

g) Tie[10] a piece of thread around the straw at this mark. (You will find it helpful to put the straws down while you do a lot of this.)

h) Tie the other end of that thread to somewhere on the second straw.

i) Hold up the second straw and slide the thread (or an owl) along, until both straws hang level. (Notice you do not have to have the owls in the grooves: they are there to stop the owls sliding off.)

j) Place[10] the mobile down, being careful to avoid tangles.

k) Now tie a thread from the second straw to the third straw, and repeat instruction i).[11]

l) Repeat instructions i), j) and k)[11] for your last straws, with the final thread forming a loop to fasten to your hook.

m) Finally,[5] hang the mobile up, and do any final sliding of threads or owls so that all the straws are level.

n) Stand back and admire your handiwork! Relax.[12]

Finding a place

✦ You will need a hook of some sort. (A drawing pin or nail will work.)

✦ The mobile will need space around it for movement.

---

7 Letters are used here as a different organisational device.

8 Adverbs are used very sparingly in this text, as the focus is kept on clarity. This one is used only because of the importance of its message.

9 Diagrams and helpful illustrations are likely to accompany an ambiguous or complicated instruction where the reader might go wrong.

10 A continued use of imperative verbs.

11 These could be very complicated directions, but references to other letters (rather than more words) ease comprehension.

12 This is an example of a single word sentence.

Understanding the grammar and punctuation

Grammar pointers

Imperative verbs

The imperative is the command form of the verb. It issues an order. The imperative form is used without a pronoun; its pronoun (the singular and plural of 'you') is simply understood. For example:

> <u>Cut</u> pieces of card.
>
> <u>Decide</u> which owls.
>
> <u>Leave</u> them to dry.

The fact that there is no written pronoun allows for shorter sentences. This is necessary when writing instructions, when clarity is so important. Consider instruction 10, and how cumbersome it immediately becomes if made into a statement and 'You will' has to be placed at the beginning.

As no pronoun is required, the imperative form can produce single word sentences. All of these, for example, are everyday orders:

> Begin.
>
> Stop.
>
> Look.

As is the example at the close of the exemplar text:

> Relax.

As well as providing brevity, imperatives also lend an air of authority to the writing, telling the reader what to do, and thereby assuming control. This is obviously ideal in this text type.

> <u>Place</u> the mobile down, being careful to avoid tangles.
>
> Now <u>tie</u> a thread from the second straw to the third straw, and <u>repeat</u> instruction i,
>
> Finally, <u>hang</u> the mobile up, and <u>do</u> any final sliding.

The imperative verb form is usually at (or near) the beginning of the sentence or clause.

> <u>Repeat</u> instruction c) for every owl.
>
> <u>Take</u> the first straw.
>
> Finally, <u>add</u> any extra features you think are needed.

Punctuation pointers

Organisational devices

These devices are an effective way of providing clarity. The subheadings 'What you need' and 'What to do' guide the reader to the appropriate place in the text, as well as informing of what is to come.

Letters and numbers are commonly used when listing instructions. They give a sequential order to the text, and separate one section from another.

> 5. Now place the tracing paper on the card, and go over those lines again, pressing firmly.
>
> 6. Remove the tracing paper, and you should be able to see your owl on the card. If the drawing isn't clear, repeat instructions.
>
> 7. Next, cut out the owl.

Bullet points, which are used at the beginning of a line, catch the eye, and command attention. Here they separate the items in a list of requirements:

- Card
- Paint
- A hole punch
- Strong thread (nylon thread will not break)
- Straws (preferably firm, plastic ones)
- Glue

Later, they are used to attract the reader's attention, and therefore stress the importance of what is being said.

- You will need a hook of some sort. (A drawing pin or nail will work.)
- The mobile will need space around it for movement.

> The children's version of these notes is on page 31 of the resource book.

The writing features of instructional texts

Structure

✦ The title must be selected with care. It needs to supply immediate information on the purpose of the text, ie what it is that is being made or done.

✦ The layout must provide clarity, with a list of the equipment needed, as here:

> *What you will need:*
>
> • *Card*
>
> • *Paint*
>
> • *A hole punch*
>
> • *Strong thread (nylon thread will not break)*
>
> • *Straws (preferably firm, plastic ones)*

✦ Chronology must be explained to the children. Talk about the need for chronological steps, so that the goal (as stated in the title) is successfully achieved. In the following examples the order of the steps is emphasised by the use of the organisational devices of numbers and letters:

> *9. Repeat instructions 4, 5, 6 and 7 until you have all your owls.*
>
> *10. Paint the owls and leave them to dry.*

and

> *j) Place the mobile down, being careful to avoid tangles.*
>
> *k) Now tie a thread from the second straw to the third straw, and repeat instruction i).*

✦ Illustrations and diagrams frequently feature in this text type. Emphasise to the children that they should be used as a reinforcement to the written instructions, bringing greater clarity and understanding to the completed text. For example, an early illustration can show the final result, and diagrams can help when words may be confusing:

> *c) Fasten some thread securely through the hole in an owl and tie it beside the groove on a straw, so that the owl dangles. (See diagram.)*

Language

Verbs

Remind the children that it is the verb that defines the tense of a sentence. The verbs in this text type have two notable features.

✦ They are generally at the beginning of the sentence.

✦ They are usually in the imperative form. (This means that they issue commands.) For example:

> *Cut pieces of card of the same size.*
>
> *Remove the tracing paper.*

The imperative form creates command sentences, and they are predominant in an instructional text. These imperative verbs are usually placed at the beginning of the sentence, although it could be interesting for the children to look at and discuss exceptions.

> *Tie the other end of that thread...* (The normal pattern is followed.)
>
> *If the drawing isn't clear, repeat instruction 5* (Here the imperative 'repeat' is at the beginning of a second clause.)
>
> *Next, cut out the owl.* (Here a time connective, 'next', is used before the verb.)

Time connectives

Connectives are link phrases or words. Time connectives are a common feature of this text type, further supporting its chronology.

> *Now place the tracing paper on the card, and go over those lines again, pressing firmly.*
>
> *Next, cut out the owl.*

These time connectives reinforce the order of the chronological steps, and act as reassurance that the correct sequence is being followed.

There are helpful hints for children on writing instructions on page 34 of the resource book.

Reports
Historical texts

Reports usually describe or classify something. They begin with a general introduction to orientate the reader, then move on to a description of particular characteristics and end with a summary. They often also include details of sources of further information and a bibliography to acknowledge sources of information.

The main difference between a report and a recount is that a report is usually non-chronological, except when the subject of the report is historical and the author needs to describe the sequence of events.

Writing a report needs careful planning, research, logical organisation and editing skills. Children need to be made aware that when they are researching a subject and then writing it up, they are in fact writing a report on the information they have found out.

Illustrations, photographs or diagrams are often included to present the information in a simplified form in order to clarify ideas.

Other features of report writing can include the use of:
✦ an impersonal third person style
✦ technical language
✦ language to describe and differentiate
✦ either the present tense or past tense, depending on the subject matter (a historical report will usually be in the past tense)
✦ the passive voice
✦ linking words and phrases, such as time connectives

Understanding the technique of report writing in the third person is important for many areas of the curriculum.

When preparing to write a report text, the author will usually make various notes during the course of the research. These can be in the form of abbreviations, symbols or diagrams.

Reports

Examples of reports

Tudors by Felicity Hebditch (Evans Brothers, 1995)

Henry, King to Be by Geoffrey Trease (Hodder/Macdonald, 1995)

Oxford Children's Book of Famous People (OUP, 1994)

Mother Teresa by Nona Morgan (Wayland, 1998)

Kings and Queens by Philip Sauvain ('Famous lives' series, Wayland, 1996)

Religions by Anita Ganeri ('Your world explained' series, Marshall Publishing, 1997)

The children's illustrated version of the notes and report is on page 41 of the resource book.

Henry VIII - notes[1]

The young Henry[2]

- *17 when king*
- *slim, good-looking then*[3]
- *Tudor men's sports (hunting, jousting)*
- *liked dancing*[4]
- *very talented musician*
- *understood languages (especially French & Latin)*
- *knew a lot (science, maths, astronomy)*

Henry's marriages

- *6*[7] *wives*
- *strange fact*
- *1st*[7] *wife – Catherine of Aragon*
- *altogether 2*[7] *divorces and 2*[7] *beheadings*
- *always wanting male heir*

Henry's children

- *lots*[9] *died at birth*
- *3 to mention: Mary (Catherine of Aragon); Elizabeth (Anne Boleyn); Edward (Jane Seymour)*
- *Edward, unhealthy, short reign*
- *Elizabeth most important: longest Tudor reign*

Henry's lifestyle as king[5]

- *liked to show off talents*
- *wore fine clothes – so he looked impressive*
- *did lots of hunting &*[6] *dancing*
- *liked tournaments &*[6] *banquets*
- *always wanted more palaces*
- *moved between palaces*
- *liked flattering portraits by best artists*

Henry's religion

- *Roman Catholic*
- *Pope (Rome) head of Church*
- *strict laws for everyone*[8]
- *no divorce – even for Henry*
- *Henry makes own Church*
- *Henry called Supreme Head of the Ch. of Eng.*
- *gets divorced*

1. Brief notes are a good way to prepare for writing an information text.

2. Using subheadings now will help with the subsequent organisation of the text.

3. Sentences are not necessary, as it is probably just the writer who needs to be able to understand the notes.

4. Bullet points are a clear, organisational device.

5. The use of subheadings is continued throughout the notes.

6. This abbreviation saves time, important when making notes.

7. It is quicker to use figures now, although the writer may prefer words later.

8. The underlining will remind the writer to stress a point in the final text.

9. There is no reason yet to think of the most appropriate language; colloquial language is good enough.

Henry VIII [10]

Henry VIII is probably the most famous of the English kings. Almost everyone knows that he had six wives, and most school history books and children's information books show portraits of a large, overdressed, middle-aged [11] figure. However, that is not the complete picture. [12]

The young Henry [13]

Henry VIII became king of England when he was only 17. Then he was a slimmer, more handsome [14] young man, who was clever and talented. His court was proud to have such a king, and he impressed the royal families of Europe. Among his impressive list of gifts he could boast:

- a talent for dancing; [15]
- a skill in sports such as hunting and jousting;
- a talented musical skill in playing, singing and composing;
- academic knowledge in the difficult fields of science, mathematics and astronomy;
- an important understanding of languages (particularly French and Latin).

Henry's lifestyle as king

Henry was keen to display these gifts. As king of England, he wore [16] finer and more expensive [14] clothes, which displayed his physique and his wealth; he held bigger and bigger tournaments and banquets; he indulged his love of hunting and dancing; he acquired the finest [17] palaces, so that he could move, indulgently, from one to another; and he made sure his grandeur was recognised by having numerous portraits of himself painted by the best [18] artists. These portraits had, of course, to be the most flattering [19] possible.

Henry's marriages [13]

We know that people remember this king because he had six [20] wives. Perhaps if his first [20] wife, Catherine of Aragon, had been able to give him a son and heir, his married life would not have resulted in this total, which is perhaps the strangest record in history. After all, [21] he was married to Catherine for 24 [20] years before he divorced her. After that, [22] this notorious count of two [20] divorces and two [20] beheadings began, all in search of a son to succeed him.

---

10 A headline gives the reader immediate understanding of what this page will be about.

11 An example of a list of adjectives separated by commas.

12 This is the writer's short introduction to the main text. It would be useful to discuss the merits of its inclusion. Could the page be better without it? Notice also that here the present tense is largely used.

13 The subheadings have been retained from the notes; they are effective divisions for the information.

14 Two comparative adjectives: the first follows the pattern of doubling the last letter and adding the suffix 'er'; but the second would sound too clumsy, and therefore needs 'more' before it.

15 Bullet points are a good organisational device. They have been used in the notes, but are also acceptable in the actual text. Remind the children that this is a text that others will use for research, and a list set out in this way gives quicker access to information that someone may be looking for.

16 This sentence is a list of statements about 'he', and is a good example of the use of semicolons. The semicolons are used instead of full stops, thereby emphasising the common theme of what would otherwise be a series of short, jerky sentences.

17 A superlative adjective which follows the normal pattern of omitting the final 'e' and adding the suffix 'est'.

18 A superlative adjective which follows the rare pattern of forming a new word.

19 A superlative adjective which follows the pattern of putting 'most' at the front.

20 There is an emphasis on numbers in this paragraph. It supports the detail and chronological accuracy of the text.

Henry's religion[23]

When Henry came to the throne, he followed the religion of England: he was a Roman Catholic. This meant that even though he was the king, he must obey even the strictest[17] laws made by the head of the Roman Catholic Church. That head was the Pope, who lived in Rome.

Divorce was against these laws of the Church, so when Henry wanted to divorce Catherine of Aragon, the Pope refused to give permission. Furious and determined to have his own way, Henry formed his own English Church and declared himself to be the Supreme Head of the Church of England.[24] That way, he could have his divorce.

Henry's children

Many of Henry's children died at the time of their birth, but not all:

1. Mary (from his marriage to Catherine of Aragon)[25]
2. Elizabeth (from his marriage to Anne Boleyn)[25]
3. Edward (from his marriage to Jane Seymour)[25]

These three names became important after Henry's death. Edward, the son he had always wanted, became king, but his health was poor and his reign short. It was his half-sister Elizabeth who was to be the most important child and to have the Tudors' longest reign. Mary, we will consider later.[26] As for Henry, he ended his life as an unhappy figure, still without the healthy male heir he wanted.[27]

21 A connective, used to help link parts of the text together.

22 A time connective, particularly important in a historical text.

23 Use is made of paragraphs in this section: the first paragraph is more general explanation, and the second provides detail of what Henry does.

24 This is an interesting sentence construction, where the description of Henry (furious and determined to have his own way) precedes the subject of the sentence (Henry).

25 This numbered list:
a) helps in the organisation and layout of the facts
b) gives chronological order

26 Notice the move from past to future tense.

27 The closing statement.

Understanding the grammar and punctuation

Grammar pointers

Adjectives

An adjective has three forms:

+ positive
+ comparative
+ superlative

The normal state is the **positive** form. For example,

> Henry was <u>keen</u>

> by having <u>numerous</u> portraits

It is only when comparisons are made that the **comparative** form is needed. For example,

> As king, he wore <u>finer</u> and <u>more expensive</u> clothes.

The comparison here is between the young prince he was and the king he has become.

There are three possible ways to form the comparative:

1. Normally, add the suffix 'er' to the adjective. Notice that spelling will often need care. For example:

   the 'y' in *wealthy* changes to 'i' before you add 'er' to become *wealthier,*

   a final consonant, as in *big*, may double before you add 'er' to become *bigger.*

2. Place 'more' in front of adjectives, usually long ones, which sound too clumsy changed according to rule 1. For example,

   > <u>more expensive</u> clothes

   > <u>more handsome</u> young man

3. Occasionally create new words. For example,

   > *good* becomes *better*

   > *bad* becomes *worse*

The **superlative** form extends the comparison to all others. It is the ultimate description of the characteristic. For example,

> a) the <u>strangest</u> record

> b) the <u>most flattering</u> portraits

> c) the <u>best</u> artists

a), b), and c) show the three possible ways to form the superlative:

1. Usually, as in a), the suffix 'est' is added to the adjective. (Again, the same spelling rules have to be observed.)
2. When this would be clumsy, as in b), 'most' is placed in front of the adjective.
3. Rarely, as in c), a new word is formed.

Punctuation pointers

Possessive apostrophes

An apostrophe can be used to denote possession. Confusion often exists about whether it is placed before or after the s which must accompany it. There are three rules:

1. Singular owners always require 's. For example,

   > Henry's religion

   > the pope's laws

2. Plural owners ending in s, just need an '.

   > the Tudors' longest reign

   > the wives' deaths

3. Plural owners not ending in s, require 's.

   > Tudor men's sports

   > women's lives

It is worth noting that in modern English, you will often see an exception to Rule 1 when the singular owner ends in s.

> King James's reign will often be written as King James' reign.

This is to avoid the clumsiness of two s sounds. Although the strict rule about where to place the apostrophe is being broken, this is now recognised as acceptable. However, there is one helpful rule for both singular and plural owners:

Place the apostrophe after the finished name of the owner.

> The children's version of these notes is on page 44 of the resource book.

The writing features of reports

Emphasise to the children that the writer must bear in mind the reason for the text: namely, to provide accurate information. Therefore, research and note-making are a likely preparation. Time devoted to these skills will be helpful.

Structure

✦ Orientation is an essential, immediate requirement. The audience needs to learn **who** was involved:

> *Henry VIII is probably the most famous of the English kings.*

when events happened:

> *Henry VIII became king of England when he was only 17.*

and **where**:

> *As king of England...*

For example, this one sentence explains all three:

> *Henry VIII became king of England*
> who   where

> *when he was only 17.*
>   when

Orientation of person (who) is evident as new sections of information are given. For example, in the section on religion:

When Henry came to the throne...

And again of person at the beginning of this paragraph:

> *Many of Henry's children died at the time of their birth*

✦ Chronology is important throughout this text type. Events are recounted in chronological order, such as here:

> *he was married to Catherine for 24 years before he divorced her. After that, this notorious count of two divorces and two beheadings began, all in search of a son to succeed him.*

Again, Henry's religious problems need to be recounted chronologically if confusion is to be avoided:

> *So when Henry wanted to divorce Catherine of Aragon, the Pope refused to give permission. Furious and determined to have his own way, Henry formed his own English Church and declared himself to be the Supreme Head of the Church of England. That way, he could have his divorce.*

✦ A closing statement brings cohesion to this text type. The ending here sums up what the audience has already learned about Henry VIII:

> *As for Henry, he ended his life as an unhappy figure, still without the healthy male heir he wanted.*

✦ Presentation is important and assists clarity in many ways. Talk to the children about:
  • Division into paragraphs
  • Headings and sub-headings
  • A helpful lay-out
  • Appropriate pictures

(Remind them that the pictures for an information text need to be accurate representations, there to add information. Draw a distinction between these and imaginative illustrations accompanying a piece of fiction.)

Language

✦ **Time connectives** are an important feature of this text type. They give further cohesion to the text:

> *After that, this notorious count of two divorces and two beheadings began, all in search of a son to succeed him.*

> *When Henry came to the throne, he followed the religion of England.*

In addition to cohesion, time connectives obviously emphasise chronology. Here it is stressed that Henry's problems did not occur immediately:

> *He was married to Catherine for 24 years before he divorced her. After that, this notorious count of two divorces and two beheadings began.*

(The time connectives are giving not just cohesion in their role as linking words, but also clarity as they stress correct chronology.)

The writing features of reports

✦ In an information text such as this, dealing with historical facts, the **third person** is likely to be used:

> *When Henry came to the throne, <u>he</u> followed the religion of England: <u>he</u> was a Roman Catholic.*

However, the **first person** also occurs, as here:

> *Mary, <u>we</u> will consider later.*

✦ The **past tense** is used in this text type:

> *Henry VIII became king of England when he was only 17. Then he was a slimmer, more handsome young man, who was clever and talented. His court was proud to have such a king, and he impressed the royal families of Europe.*

However, the opening paragraph of the exemplar is in the present tense; and the penultimate sentence of the text is in the future tense. Discuss with the children the reasons for this. (In the first paragraph, the writer is introducing the subject; the sentence about Mary links to a later section of the book.)

There are helpful hints for children on writing an information text on page 47 of the resource book.

Explanation texts 1

The purpose of an explanation text is to explain how or why something works, or how or why something happens. They are written as if in response to a question, and indeed a question often makes the best title for this text type.

A good explanation can deceive by its apparent simplicity. It presents information clearly, establishing one point before moving on to the next. In reality, the simplicity is not achieved without meticulous planning, for information must be presented in the correct order, if an explanation is to be readily understood.

For example, a writer may be presenting a complicated scientific process to an audience of laymen who know little about the subject: background information is needed; technical vocabulary must be defined; and finally the complete question must be answered. Without a planned order, in the form of a logical series of steps, the explanation merely brings confusion.

This order and clarity can be assisted in many ways: an effective division into paragraphs; the use of organisational devices such as subheadings, numbered lists and bullet points; a reliance on illustrations and diagrams; and an effective use of language. All these add to the appeal and accessibility of the explanation, making it an efficient source of research.

However, content must not be compromised for appearance. Although a clear layout is helpful, at every point the primary purpose of this non-fiction text type must be kept in mind: namely, to explain.

Explanation texts

Examples of explanation texts

You and your body by Susan Meredith, Kate Needham and Mike Unwin ('Starting Point' series, Usborne, 1996)

How do we move? by Carol Ballard ('How our bodies work' series, Wayland, 1997)

My Big Question and Answer Book (Kingfisher, 2000)

How the Universe Works by Heather Couper and Nigel Henbest ('Eye Witness' series, Dorling Kindersley, 1994)

Personal Stereo by Catherine Chambers ('Look Inside' series, Heinemann Library, 1998)

Machines by Chris Oxlade ('Investigations' series, Lorenz Books, 2001)

Electricity by Steve Parker ('Eye Witness' series, Dorling Kindersley, 1992)

The Lightbulb by Michael Pollard ('History and Invention' series, Simon and Schuster Young Books, 1994)

The children's version of the explanation is on page 54 of the resource book.

How does an electric circuit work?[1]

An electric circuit is the path electricity follows. For even the simplest electrical device to work, there has to be a complete circuit.[2]

Essential requirements[3]
1) a source of electricity[4]
2) materials that **conduct**[5] electricity (materials that allow electricity to flow through them)[5]

These are[6] the most important parts of any electrical circuit, but **insulating**[7] materials (materials that do not allow electricity to flow through them)[7] are[6] also in a circuit. Their roles are demonstrated[6] in this simple classroom experiment.

Lighting up[8]

Diagram 1[8]

This diagram shows an example of a complete circuit made in a classroom experiment. First,[10] the battery, a safe source of electricity, is selected.[11] Then,[10] because metal is known[11] to be a material that conducts electricity, thin wires are chosen.[11] After that,[10] the metal end of one wire makes a secure connection with the metal of the screw in the bulb holder, with its other end touching the **positive**[12] metal end of the battery (marked +).[12]

[13]When that is done, the second[14] wire mirrors the process: the other metal screw and the **negative**[12] end of the battery (marked −)[12] are connected. Because[15] all these parts are included, the circuit is complete, so[15] the bulb lights up. If[15] just one connection comes loose, the circuit is incomplete, and so[15] the light goes out.

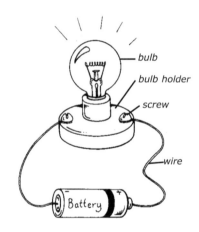

Diagram 1[9]

labels: bulb, bulb holder, screw, wire, Battery

1 An explanation text is commonly the response to a question asking How?/Why? The question makes a suitable title for the explanation.

2 A short statement to introduce the topic.

3 A subheading is an organisational device that helps give a clear layout to the text.

4 A numbered list is another effective organisational device.

5 The word is highlighted and then defined. Comprehension of this word is clearly important to the topic.

6 The present tense is the usual tense for explanations.

7 Again the importance of understanding certain vocabulary is stressed. Notice that the author is supplying these basic definitions as an early step in the explanation.

8 Subheadings are helpful, not just in layout, but also for scanning the text.

9 Diagrams and illustrations are commonly used, with labelling as needed.

10 Time connectives give the chronology of the process.

11 Again verbs are in the present tense; they are also in the passive voice. This is common in explanations, and gives an impersonal tone to the writing.

12 A potentially difficult word is explained with its symbol.

13 A new paragraph is begun here to allow one set of information to be digested before moving on to the next step. A series of steps is often apparent in this text type.

14 Chronological order is further emphasised by this reference to number.

15 The use of cause and effect phrases is a common feature of explanations.

Diagram 2[16]

This diagram shows the experiment being repeated, but dispensing with the bulb holder. <u>In order to make</u>[15] the bulb light now, two points of contact on the bulb must be reached:

<u>1) the metal stud at the bottom of the bulb</u>[4]

<u>2) the metal screw thread of the bulb</u>[4]

The wires must touch these two places for the bulb to light up. The screw thread and stud are separated by <u>insulating</u>[18] material. Again, both wires and both ends of the battery need to be in place <u>so that</u>[15] a complete circuit is made.

Points to remember[19]

<u>1) Electricity flows in a circuit.</u>[20]
<u>2) That circuit is a continuous path.</u>[20]
<u>3) Any break in the circuit interferes with the flow.</u>[20]
<u>4) If the circuit breaks, the electrical device cannot work.</u>[20]

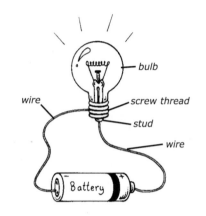

bulb
wire
screw thread
stud
wire
Battery

Diagram 2[17]

16 The text moves to a more complicated step, hence the new paragraph and the new subheading.

17 The diagram is a useful aid to understanding this part of the text.

18 Here a word (insulating) is used after being defined early in the text. The importance and usefulness of such defining of technical vocabulary becomes obvious.

19 An effective subheading, helpful and attracting the eye if scanning.

20 The numbered list is a clear way to set out the points, as well as suggesting an order of importance.

Understanding the grammar and punctuation

Grammar pointers

Verbs

Explanation texts are written in the present tense.

> *First, the battery, a safe source of electricity, is selected. Then, because metal is known to be a material that conducts electricity, thin wires are chosen.*

It is worth noting that many of these verbs are written in the passive voice (ie where the person or thing is acted upon by the verb). This makes the writing more impersonal, and is more appropriate for explanation texts. Compare the way the verbs are used above with how they are used below:

> <u>we select</u> a battery

> <u>I choose</u> thin wires

The active form of the verbs has been used. Immediately, the tone has become conversational, less knowledgeable, less appropriate and far less effective.

Punctuation pointers

Subheadings

Subheadings are an organisational device. 'Sub' is the Latin for 'below', and these are headings that come below the main heading. They fulfil many functions:

✦ The structure of the text is helped. Subheadings can be a good way to ensure that the explanation avoids becoming a confusing mixture of text and diagrams. Here it is clear where to look next on the page:

> *Diagram 1*

✦ The layout gains appeal. The text becomes more approachable and manageable because of this structure. For example:

> *Essential requirements*

This offers the audience reassurance that the explanation will begin at a basic level.

✦ Accessibility is given to the audience by this labelling of different sections of the text. It is easier to identify the steps being taken in the explanation and where to find each.

✦ Signposts are created by subheadings, giving advance knowledge of what is to come. For example:

> *Diagram 2*

This may prompt movement to that section of the text, if the relevant, desired diagram has already been identified.

✦ Scanning becomes an attractive and useful possibility. Here the audience can quickly move to a summary, again saving time:

> *Points to remember*

Numbered and bulleted lists

A numbered or bulleted list is another organisational device, again providing many advantages.

✦ Its layout on separate lines makes the explanation much clearer, such as here, when the two parts of the bulb are numbered in this way:

> *1) the metal stud at the bottom of the bulb*

> *2) the metal screw thread of the bulb*

✦ Scanning a list such as this is easier than scanning a wordy paragraph. The numbered list at the end of the exemplar is particularly useful.

✦ Simplification is often added to the explanation by the reduction in words that may be gained from using this organisational device. Here the writer dispenses with the need for a full sentence when using a list:

> *Essential requirements*

> *1) a source of electricity*

> *2) materials that **conduct** electricity (materials that allow electricity to flow through them)*

✦ An order of importance is implied in the above list, but a numbered list can be useful when stressing a definite chronological order, or numbering a series of steps in the explanation.

Understanding the grammar and punctuation

◆ Visual digits help in the final list, where not only
has the writer probably put the points in order of
importance, but is also helping the audience to
scan and absorb the information and the fact that
there are four points, by using numbers:

Points to remember

1) Electricity flows in a circuit.

2) That circuit is a continuous path.

3) Any break in the circuit interferes with the flow.

*4) If the circuit breaks, the electrical device cannot
work.*

The children's version of these notes is on
page 56 of the resource book.

The writing features of explanation texts

Explain to the children that they need to understand the answer to the question before trying to explain it to others. Checking facts and doing research will be needed. Careful planning of the presentation is vital. Work with them on how to plan their writing in a series of steps, where to include diagrams and so on.

Structure

The opening statement
This should be concise. Here it is kept short and introduces the text:

An electric circuit is the path electricity follows.

As the audience must know what an electric circuit is before an explanation about how an one works can be given, the introduction is simply that opening statement, followed by a comment on the need for complete circuits:

An electric circuit is the path electricity follows. For even the simplest electrical device to work, there has to be a complete circuit.

Logical and chronological order
Remind the children that they must assume the audience knows little about the subject. Therefore the answer needs to be given one step at a time; a series of steps is often apparent in an explanation.

For example, the circuit using a bulb holder (Diagram 1) is explained before the one without (Diagram 2). Likewise, the essential requirements are given before the diagrams are explained:

Essential requirements

1) a source of electricity

*2) materials that **conduct** electricity (materials that allow electricity to flow through them)*

*These are the most important parts of any electrical circuit, but **insulating** materials (materials that do not allow electricity to flow through them)...*

A logical order here has been emphasised by the use of a numbered list.

Technical information
Important definitions or additional pieces of information are best supplied as an early step in the explanation. For example:

*2) materials that **conduct** electricity (materials that allow electricity to flow through them)*

Diagrams and pictures
These are a common feature of explanations. Emphasise to the children that their link to a certain part of the text must be clear, perhaps by a reference, such as 'See Diagram 1'. Diagrams may also require their own subheadings or labels.

Language

Time connectives
An explanation text, because of its emphasis on chronological order, makes frequent use of time connectives. (These are linking words or phrases associated with time.) For example:

<u>First,</u> the battery, a safe source of electricity, is selected. <u>Then,</u> because metal is known to be a material that conducts electricity, thin wires are chosen. <u>After that</u>...

Cause and effect phrases
These are useful language tools, drawing together an action and its effect and emphasising mutual dependence. This text contains numerous examples:

<u>Because</u> all these parts are included, the circuit is complete, <u>so</u> the bulb lights up.

There are helpful hints for children on writing an explanation on page 59 of the resource book.

Explanation texts 2

Explanations deal with processes. Their purpose is to explain how or why something happens. The tone of the text is impersonal. It is a text type where clarity and clear information form the focus. Intrusion by the author, therefore, is inappropriate. For this reason, use of the third person is correct. Any references to people are general, with the text focusing on a process, as opposed to describing an individual following the steps of the process.

The tone is also formal. The absence of personal involvement or specific people promotes this. In addition, use of the passive voice can contribute to this formality: the air of detachment is continued, and a desired tone of authority is added. However, this authority must be supported by sufficient knowledge; to this end, careful planning is essential, of both the information and the sequence it follows.

Language also affects tone. Although technical terms must be used, clear definitions must somehow be made accessible to the layman. Therefore, in this text type there is a requirement for a balance between technical, not simplified, terminology and clarity. Causal and sequential connectives can contribute here, by making the meaning of an explanation clear, with their emphasis on logic and a time-related order.

Finally, a suitable tone is achieved by presentation. Layout, division into paragraphs, organisational features, and diagrams and flow charts all contribute to a text which presents an authoritative explanation, yet also offers the necessary accessibility to its audience.

Explanations

Examples of explanations

Making Shoes ('Making' series, Franklin Watts, 1986)

Glass by Jane Chandler ('Threads' series, A&C Black, 1992)

It's Metal ('A Material World' series, Wayland, 1992)

Paper by Henry Pluckrose ('Find Out About' series, Franklin Watts, 1997)

New Energy Sources by Nigel Hawkes (Aladdin Books, 2000)

Energy by Robin Kerrod ('Get an insight into' series, OUP, 1993)

Internet and E-mail by Chris Oxlade (Heinemann Library Books, Reed Educational and Professional Publishing, 2001)

The children's illustrated version of the explanation is on page 66 of the resource book.

Making glass bottles

Glass bottles are[2] made in a factory called a glassworks. They are[2] the product of a stone combination.[3]

What is the stone combination?[4]

The usual stones combined[5] are:

1.[6]	sand	4.[6]	alumina
2.[6]	sodium carbonate	5.[6]	salt cake
3.[6]	limestone	6.[6]	minor ingredients

The proportions may vary, but are likely to be in the region of 70%[7] sand, 15%[7] sodium carbonate, 10%[7] limestone, 4%[7] alumina, 0.9%[7] salt cake and 0.1%[7] of other minor ingredients. Once crushed, these stones are mixed[8] together, then melted[8] in large ovens which operate at temperatures above 1,500°C[7]. The heat must be intense in order that melting points are reached. Once[9] the stones are crushed, combined and melted, clear glass is finally[9] produced.

Decorative glass[10]

As for[11] decorative glass, additional material is required in the manufacturing. Lead glass has an attractive, distinctive sparkle to it. However,[12] this is only achieved because[13] of the addition of lead to the crushed and melted mixture. Similar additions are necessary so that[13] coloured glass may be produced:

a) if[13] a small amount of nickel is used, then[13] the glass becomes yellow;

b) and as a result of[13] adding a little gold, glass becomes red.

The melted mixture[14]

The hot, melted mixture falls into a tube. From this tube, the flow is then directed into iron bottle moulds,[15] which are being carried along a conveyor-belt. After this,[16] the mould is carried under pipes pumping out cold air. At this stage,[16] cold air is directed onto the mould; therefore,[17] the glass mixture begins to lose heat.

The final product[18]

During this process of temperature reduction, the glass takes on the shape of the bottle mould. However,[19] in order to[20] gain strength, the bottle must be finally[21] heated up again and cooled. At last, it is ready to be used.[22]

See the next page for a flow chart[23] showing the process described above.

---

1 An explanation text can describe a process.
2 Verbs are in the present tense.
3 The first paragraph forms a short, general introduction to the topic.
4 A subheading introduces the new paragraph, supplying a clear separation of the text and also informing the audience of what is to follow. A question, which can then be answered, is a practical subheading.
5 There is an obvious link with the last subheading where the words 'stone combination' were used.
6 Numbers help to separate the items in a list more clearly, as well as suggesting a ranking order.
7 Facts, figures and correct technical terms are important in this text type.
8 The passive is used frequently in explanations, as it provides a formal, impersonal tone.
9 Time connectives stress the correct sequence of the process.
10 A new paragraph is needed because a new area of the subject is to be looked at.
11 A connective phrase eases the move to a new paragraph.
12 The connective introduces a surprising or exceptional point.
13 Cause and effect connectives feature prominently in this text type.
14 The subheading informs the audience of what is to come.
15 Correct technical terms are important.
16 Sequential connectives play an important role in emphasising correct order of the steps of the process, as well as providing smooth links between parts of the text.
17 An emphatic causal connective.
18 A clear subheading informs the audience that the process is almost complete.
19 The connective introduces an unexpected point.
20 A cause and effect link phrase.
21 The adverb confirms that this is the last step in the process.
22 An effective concluding sentence, reaffirming that the bottle is now ready.
23 A flow chart clarifies points made in the text, as well as emphasising the correct order of the process.

Understanding the grammar and punctuation

Grammar pointers

Paragraphs
A paragraph is one section in a piece of writing. It tends to be about one specific aspect of the topic under consideration.

They always begin on a new line and sometimes that first line is indented.

Beginning new paragraphs
A new paragraph begins because of a change in the writing. Possible changes include:
- Time
- Place
- Issue
- Focus
- Speaker

For example, a new paragraph is begun here as the focus changes, moving away from a general introduction to specific detail:

> What is the stone combination?
>
> The usual combination is...

The function of paragraphs
- They assist the writer in the organisation of thoughts.
- They assist the audience in the comprehension of those thoughts.
- They improve presentation, by making the layout of the text clearer.

Link phrases
Link phrases are groups of words that link different parts of a text. They maintain the cohesion of the text. For example, the phrase at the start of the following sentence helps to link the new paragraph to the preceding one:

> _As for_ decorative glass...

(Notice that the link phrase at the beginning of the sentence improves the flow of the text.)

Cause and effect
In explanation texts, link phrases are often about cause and effect. For example, the exemplar explains that the combination of stone materials can melt as an effect of high temperatures. The link phrase emphasises that:

> The heat must be intense, _in order that_ melting points are reached.

Similarly, the following link phrase emphasises that the glass's colour is caused by the addition of gold:

> _As a result of_ adding a little gold, glass becomes red.

Sequence
Time link phrases are particularly relevant to this text type. As an explanation is written as a series of steps, so sequential link phrases are likely to form a prominent feature. They fulfil two functions:
1) they link parts of the text;
2) they stress the correct order of a process.

For example:

> _After this,_ the mould is carried under pipes pumping out cold air. _At this stage,_ cold air is directed onto the mould;
>
> _At last,_ it is ready to be used.

Punctuation pointers

Connectives
'Connectives' is the generic term for link phrases and single linking words used to connect writing.

Along with commas and full stops, connectives are used to join clauses to make sentences. A well-chosen connective often proves the most effective link at a particular point.

The most common connectives in this text type are causal connectives and sequential connectives.

Causal connectives
These connectives focus on logic, dealing with cause and effect. For example:

> _if_ a small amount of nickel is used, _then_ the glass becomes yellow;
>
> _therefore,_ the glass mixture begins to lose heat.

Sequential connectives
These connectives are concerned with time and the sequence of events – an essential emphasis in this text type:

> _Once_ crushed, these stones are mixed together, _then_ melted in large ovens...
>
> _Once_ the stones are crushed, combined and melted, clear glass is _finally_ produced.

Understanding the grammar and punctuation

It is worth looking at this sentence:

> _However, this is only achieved because of the addition of lead to the crushed and melted mixture._

'However' is a connective of opposition, introducing an opposing or unusual point. Notice that connectives such as this conjunction, placed almost independently at the start of a sentence, normally have a comma after them. Commas are likely to feature in any sentence where connectives are employed. For example:

> _However, in order to gain strength, the bottle must be finally heated up again and cooled._

Reading sentences aloud will help the children to identify if and where commas are needed.

> The children's version of these notes is on page 68 of the resource book.

Writing features of explanation texts

Structure

Opening statement
Remind the children to keep this to a general introduction to the topic.

Presentation
Presentation is a key issue in this text type. Remind the children to be aware of issues such as:
- layout, involving helpful positioning of the text;
- diagrams and illustrations, labelled as needed;
- headings and subheadings, acting as useful markers for different sections of the explanation;
- bullet points, clear attention-grabbers;
- letters, a separation of different points;
- numbers, placing an emphasis on sequence.

Sequential order
An explanation is a series of steps. Therefore content, presentation and language reflect this. The answer to the title needs to be given one step at a time, but these steps must be in the right order.

Language

Sequential connectives
The focus on sequence in an explanation means that sequential connectives are a common feature. Words such as *after* and *finally* are used. The intention is to make the different steps in the process clear. For example:

> <u>Once</u> the stones are crushed, combined and melted, clear glass is <u>finally</u> produced.

Paragraphs
Paragraphs also supply this sequential order. The paragraphs can do this in a number of ways:

- A paragraph is a distinct, discrete section of the text, and by moving to a new one, the writer is signalling a change of content. In other words, one step of the explanation is complete, and the next is being moved to; for example, the move from 'The melted mixture' to 'The final product'.
- Linking words or phrases ease the flow of the text between paragraphs. Use of particular words or phrases helps to maintain the cohesion of the explanation, thereby keeping a link between the steps in the process. For example:

> *after; at this stage; then; once*

Causal connectives
These cause and effect words are similarly important. Remind the children of different examples, with these likely to be particularly useful:

> *as a result; therefore; because; in order to*

Tone
The tone of an explanation is formal. The explanation must be written in a way that sounds both clear and knowledgeable; a casual, friendly tone fails to inspire this confidence. The correct tone is gained in a number of ways:
- Technical vocabulary – correct terms need to be used. Simplified terms are not acceptable; nevertheless, clear definitions need to be supplied.
- The use of the third person (rather than an informal first person) brings authority to the writing. An explanation is about a process, not about an individual; therefore, references to any people are non-specific.
- There may be occasions when the passive voice is more appropriate than the active voice. A passive construction further adds gravity to the tone of the text. For example:

> *Once crushed...* (This gives a more formal, authoritative tone than the active version: after someone crushed them.)

The same is true here:

> *The usual stones combined are* (passive)

> *The usual stones we combine are* (active)

Look for other examples and discuss them with the children.

Verbs
Explanation texts are generally written in the present tense, as the process being explained is one that keeps on happening. Stress to the children the need to keep to this tense.

> There are helpful hints for children on writing an explanation text on page 71 of the resource book.

Advertisements

Advertisements have a definite goal: to persuade. The text aims to seize the audience's attention, sway it with its claims, and achieve a desired end. Information and facts are there, but the arguments and views are one-sided, and the claims are often exaggerated. Presentation of these is the key to the text's success.

Layout is not accidental. An audience must be drawn to the advertisement. Bold lettering and punctuation may catch the eye; a picture can trigger a response; unusual shapes will lead the audience to important messages; a final instruction may find just the right angle on the page to be noticed. Colour also plays an essential part, with the writer recognising the associations and feelings it arouses.

Language, likewise, plays a leading role: not only punctuation, but also words are dramatic. Use is made of alliteration and onomatopoeia; jingles and slogans are devised; rhymes are concocted; puns are used; and words are even invented. Vocabulary is often emotive, with the exact word matched to the target audience. The advertisement must persuade, and it will seem to be talking directly to YOU.

Persuasive texts

Examples of persuasive texts

✦ Collect a range of advertisements from the printed media for comparison and discussion.

✦ Food packaging, such as crisp packets.

✦ Notes on television advertisements that have catchy jingles.

✦ Notes on advertisements seen on hoardings.

Advertising ('Media Story' series, Wayland, 1990)

Advertising by David Lusted ('Points of View' series, Wayland, 1991)

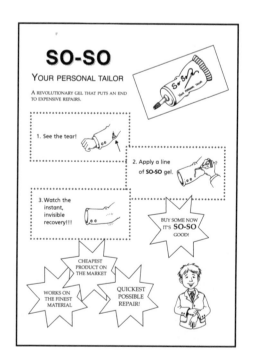

The children's version of the advertisements is on page 78 of the resource book.

Advertisements

How would YOU describe this puppy?[1]

Helpless?[3]

Appealing?[3]

Loveable?[3]

Playful?[3]

This is what <u>somebody</u>[4] thought of Sandy:

- <u>Worthless</u>[5] – he had been left without food and water for days.

- <u>Dangerous</u>[5] – he had been cruelly muzzled and tied up.

- <u>Objectionable</u>[5] – at six weeks he was covered with livid bruises and open sores from vicious kicks and beatings.

- <u>Disposable</u>[5] – he had been left completely abandoned in a disused warehouse.

2

<u>**Help us find the other desperate dogs.**</u>[6]
<u>**Together we**[7] **can do it!**</u>[6]
<u>**If you care, please give generously.**</u>[6]
Donations to: Dogged Defence
5 Woofcroft Road, Haxby
Coventry CV8 1FH

<u>MONEY = RESCUE</u>[8]

BLOCS[9]

THE NEW FOOTBALL-SHAPED SNACK

<u>Sweet, sugary, scrumptious</u>[12] balls of chocolate

<u>Crunchy, crackling, crispy</u>[12] centres

<u>Get your palate-changing</u>[13] experience <u>NOW!</u>[14]

10

Collect your full <u>England squad – a player's name inside every wrapper.</u>[15]

---

1 A question directly to the audience, by the use of YOU, gives involvement.

2 The picture of a dog is likely to have strong, emotional appeal, and therefore is a very good beginning.

3 These adjectives are likely to correspond to those in the audience's mind.

4 The 'somebody' is not on the right side, and not one of us.

5 Adjectives that compare unfavourably with the attractive ones at the start.

6 These are emotive messages.

7 The concept of the audience and advertisement being on the same (good) side – 'we' – is reinforced.

8 The symbol = gives variety, and allows for quick explanation of a point.

9 This attracts attention because of its peculiar spelling. (Perhaps it should be BLOCKS or CHOCS?)

10 Target market addressed in picture of a child.

11 A catchy rhyme is used to get the product's name remembered.

12 Examples of alliteration.

13 An exaggerated claim, typical of advertisements.

14 A need to buy immediately in capitalised use of this word.

15 This is an extra incentive to buy; this is often seen in advertisements.

SO-SO [16]

YOUR PERSONAL TAILOR [16]

A REVOLUTIONARY GEL THAT PUTS AN END
TO EXPENSIVE REPAIRS

1.   See the tear!

2.   Apply a line
of **SO-SO** gel.

3. Watch the
instant,
invisible
recovery!!!

BUY
SOME NOW!
IT'S **SO-SO**
GOOD!

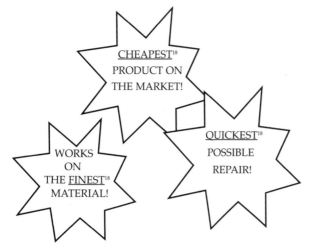

CHEAPEST [18]
PRODUCT ON
THE MARKET!

WORKS
ON
THE FINEST [18]
MATERIAL!

QUICKEST [18]
POSSIBLE
REPAIR!

17

16 The two words make the pun
clear: ie SO-SO is a play on
'sew'.

17 Pictures allow a quick
understanding of the whole
process.

18 Superlatives are commonly
used.

WANTED![19]

Boys and Girls[20]
Ages 8-12[20]

Do YOU[21] HAVE THESE?
- BASIC BALL SKILLS
- EXTRA ENERGY
- AGILE ABILITY
- A WILL TO WIN

Then we've been searching for YOU![21]

Our Soccer Summer School is from August 10th to August 17th this year. It's a one-week, residential course at Littlehall, famed for the finest facilities and most experienced F A coaches.[22]

WE OFFER:

My star player has learned to control a ball in a way I can only dream of.

- **Supreme skills**[23]
FA coaches train you in small groups, leaving you with the skills of the greatest players.[24]

Grab your place! This is the best under-11 coaching scheme I've ever seen.[25]

It was great! I loved every moment of last year's course, and have begged for a return trip.

- **Penalty precision practice**[23]
We prepare you for a game's tensest moments.

This is one of the places I visit every summer scouting for future talent.

- **Physical fitness**[23]
The programme is tailored to your individual needs and is designed to take you to the highest levels of fitness.

I've always been a tomboy, but this was the best thing ever. Just wait until the boys in the park take me on now!

- **Winning ways**[23]
Visiting Premier League players tell you how to get to the top.[24]

It was worth every penny!

They're really patient with you. Now I feel I can keep up with the best at school.

LET OUR DREAM TEAM WORK ON YOU![26]
PLACES LIMITED • BOOK EARLY!
APPLY NOW![27]

Applications by phone or letter:
Summer Training School, Littlehall Centre, Coxford, SOMERSET
BR2 RS1. Tel. 0800 453127

I've been for the last two years. It's got me off the bench to a regular first team place.

19 It carries an urgent message, both in the word itself and by the punctuation after it; therefore, it is an effective start.

20 The desired audience is immediately targeted.

21 YOU gives a personal, direct approach.

22 Further detail is only given once the audience is captive.

23 Emphasis added by alliteration.

24 These are impossible claims, but a child is unlikely to think very logically about them.

25 Good, informed opinions will help to convince.

26 Example of assonance.

27 Final exhortation, given urgency by word NOW and the use of a dramatic exclamation mark.

Understanding the grammar and punctuation

Understanding the grammar and punctuation enables children to control the language they use and therefore to write more interesting and powerful advertisements.

Grammar pointers

Adjectives
Adjectives are describing words. They qualify the nouns or pronouns in a sentence, adding detail to them. For example:

> A <u>REVOLUTIONARY</u> GEL THAT PUTS AN END TO <u>EXPENSIVE</u> REPAIRS

> a <u>disused</u> warehouse

> It was <u>great</u>!

Types of adjectives
There are many ways to classify adjectives. In the exemplar, some deal with:

- facts

  disused, residential, visiting

- emotions

  appealing, loveable

- taste

  sweet, sugary, scrumptious

- time

  quickest, instant

Numerous other possible groups could include: colour, mood, size and texture.

Superlative adjectives
A superlative adjective is the highest form of an adjective. It describes its strongest degree of intensity. For example:

> WORKS ON THE <u>FINEST</u> MATERIAL!

> <u>QUICKEST</u> POSSIBLE REPAIR!

> <u>CHEAPEST</u> PRODUCT ON THE MARKET!

The formation of superlative adjectives:

1. The superlative is usually formed by adding 'est' to the basic adjective. Therefore,

   quick becomes *quickest*

   cheap becomes *cheapest*

Sometimes a final 'e' may need to disappear. For example:

> *fine* becomes *finest*

> *late* becomes *latest*

2. With a longer adjective, a final 'est' may make the sound too clumsy. Therefore 'most' is put at the front:

   experienced becomes *most experienced*

   patient becomes *most patient*

3. A new word is occasionally formed:

   good becomes *best*

   bad becomes *worst*

Punctuation pointers

Exclamation marks
An exclamation mark looks like this !. It may follow an interjection, or end a sentence. It indicates great emotion, such as joy, anger, surprise, humour, pain, shock or urgency.

> *It was great!*

> *Grab your place!*

Dashes
A dash looks like this –. A dash may be used to introduce another piece of information, replacing other punctuation marks in informal writing, and to indicate an afterthought. For example:

> *Collect your full England squad – a player's name inside every wrapper.*

> *Worthless – he had been left without food and water for days.*

Dashes are also used in pairs – like brackets – to insert a piece of information. For example, the text could have read:

> *Collect your full England squad – with a player's name inside every wrapper – from your local shop.*

Understanding the grammar and punctuation

Colons

A colon looks like this :. It introduces information.
The information follows logically from the first part of
the sentence. For example:

Donations to: Dogged Defence

That information is often a list. For example:

WE OFFER:

- *Penalty precision practice*

- *Physical fitness*

Bullet points

A bullet point looks like this •. Bullet points are often
used in lists, to help in the organisation of the items,
clearly separating one from another. This use is clear
in the last example, and again here:

DO YOU HAVE THESE?

- *BASIC BALL SKILLS*

- *EXTRA ENERGY*

The children's version of these notes is on
page 81 of the resource book.

The writing features of advertisements

Emphasise to the children that the purpose of an advertisement is to persuade. Every element – appearance, language, illustration and punctuation – works towards that end.

Structure

Gaining attention

The advertisement must catch the eye, and initial impact must be made by a picture or a word. The exemplar texts often combine both, using dramatic punctuation as well. For example:

> *WANTED!*

Another effective opening could be a question. For example:

> *Do you care?*

> *Like sweets?*

> *Care for a game?*

All these could be matched effectively to the exemplar texts. In all cases, the audience is being asked to stop and think.

Layout

Focus on the benefits brought by variety. You should use all the elements of the advertisement:

- **Print**
  Letters may vary in size and type, pushing the audience towards the most important word(s). For example:

  > *Then we've been searching for YOU!*

  Inevitably, YOU commands attention.

- **Positioning**
  Parts of the text may be placed at different orientations and in unusual places in the advertisement. The audience notices them because of this.

- **Boxes/Shapes**
  Similarly, the use of a text box or a circle can make that part of the advertisement noticeable. For example:

  > *Collect your full England squad – a player's name inside every wrapper.*

This text has been put at the bottom, in a curly cloud, almost as a postscript. The audience will be curious to find out what it says.

- **Symbols**
  Symbols such as ticks, crosses and mathematical signs bring an efficient shorthand to this text type. For example:

  > *MONEY = RESCUE*

- **Speech bubbles**
  Again these provide variety in the appearance and structure of the text. In addition, they are effective as a means of supporting the claims of the advertisement, particularly when an authoritative source is being quoted.

  > *Grab your place! This is the best under-11 coaching scheme I've ever seen.*

- **Illustrations**
  These can be effective at every stage: attracting attention, explaining the text and reinforcing the message.

  This is very clear in the So-So advertisement, where the way to apply the gel is shown, as well as its pleasing results.

  Similarly, in the Dogged Defence case, the audience will be drawn back to the attractive picture of the helpless puppy, and will be persuaded to be generous.

- **Colour**
  This can be an important factor. Colours have certain connotations. For example:
  - Green has environmental links;
  - Blue is cool;
  - Red is dangerous;
  - Yellow is warm and sunny, and so on.

  Consequently, moods and attitudes can be affected by the choice of colour. Words can be made to stand out.

  Talk to the children about how to gain benefits from selective use of colour.

There are helpful hints for children on writing an advertisement on page 84 of the resource book.

Discussion texts

The purpose of this text type is to present every side of a discussion. It must allow a view of all aspects of an issue, as different opinions are represented and various viewpoints are put forward.

First the issue must be clearly identified; then the ensuing text must represent a balance of the opinions about that issue. Debate may be passionate with views often widely apart. The arguments for and against the issue are likely to be expressed emotively and language used manipulatively. Therefore, the choice of words and the manner in which parts of the text are linked make an important contribution to the success of the arguments. Logical connectives not only improve the flow of the text but also strengthen arguments by making them seem more plausible.

An argument needs to be constructed with care, with evidence and examples cited to support the particular stance. In the same way, general, non-specific references to an indefinite number of individuals holding the same view can make an opinion sound more widely held than is actually the case. Further strength is gained by the use of the present tense, which conveys urgency and passion.

A discussion text ends by summarising the points made, and bringing the writing to a rational conclusion. The text will succeed in making the issue clearer; it will allow a balanced view to be taken; and it will help in reaching a decision.

The ability to write discussion texts is an extension of persuasive writing. If one side of an argument can be put well, then so can both sides.

Discussion texts

Examples of discussion texts

Vegetarianism by Samantha Calvert ('We're Talking About' series, Wayland, 1997)

Animal Rights by Anita Ganeri ('What's the Big Idea?' series, Hodder, 1997)

Animal Welfare by Jillian Powell ('What do we think about?' series, Wayland, 1999)

The Environment and You by Alexander Gray ('What's at issue?' series, Heinemann Library Books, Reed Educational & Professional Publishing, 2000)

Stand up for your rights (Two-Can Publishing, 1998)

The children's version of the text is on page 91 of the resource book.

<u>For or against?</u>[1]
<u>Will the pupils of Free-For-All School be compelled</u>
<u>to wear a uniform?</u>[2]

The fourth in our series of how local issues affect the community

By your local reporter

Alisha Sakram

<u>Since Free-For-All School opened 25 years ago, it has always followed a no-uniform policy. This newspaper knows that many parents select this secondary school entirely because of this relaxed approach.</u>[3]

<u>However,</u>[4] Cynthia Fussdom, the new headmistress, is demanding change, as shown in the newsletter that she sent to all parents on 5 March which reads:

To All Parents

After observing my pupils for six months, I <u>must</u>[5] finally express my <u>deep</u>[6] concern over the <u>low</u>[6] standards of dress of many of them. Fashion <u>is overriding</u>[7] good sense; sensible, practical clothes are absent; and <u>appalling</u>[6] taste is evident.

In the last week alone, I have observed:
- <u>So-called 'mini-skirts'</u>[8]
- <u>Creased, faded trousers (apparently referred to as 'distressed')</u>
- <u>Shoes with kitten heels</u>
- <u>Heavy, boot-like footwear</u>
- <u>T-shirts that are far too tight and</u>

<u>short for their wearers.</u>

<u>Therefore,</u>[9] in September this year, a smart, grey and black school uniform will be introduced for every pupil in the school.

Your full cooperation in this matter <u>is expected.</u>[10]

The repercussions have been swift and strong. There is an on-going war of words, and Friday's sit-down protest outside the school shows the depth of the feelings aroused.

These letters are merely a <u>sample</u>[11] from our postbag.

---

12 Bullimore Grove
Stringley

Dear Miss Fussdom

Horrified, I <u>hold</u>[12] a directive from you, which <u>demands</u>[12] that my 14-year-old daughter <u>attires</u>[12] herself in <u>drab garments</u>[13] reminiscent of the <u>Victorian age.</u>[13]

How dare you! You are a newcomer to our community, and cannot be allowed to destroy the free spirit of our school. Many revere Free-For-All <u>because</u>[14] of its lack of uniform, and no upstart can change this.

Our children maintain the right to be themselves, and, <u>therefore,</u>[15] I am helping like-minded

1 The heading indicates a two-sided discussion.

2 The subheading supplies specific details, and states briefly the issue involved.

3 This paragraph is used to give a fuller, clearer statement of the issue.

4 This logical connective links the preceding attitude to Miss Fussdom's opposing viewpoint.

5 Strong emphatic verb stresses depth of the writer's feelings.

6 These feelings are further emphasised by emotional, probably exaggerated, epithets.

7 The present tense is usual in this text type.

8 A detailed list is used as evidence to support an opinion.

9 A logical connective links the evidence to the decision.

10 The choice of the present tense strengthens the statement. (Compare a weaker version: 'will be expected'.)

11 Arguments from both sides should be in this sample; an equal balance is required in this text type.

12 The present tense conveys immediacy and drama.

13 Emotive, almost hysterical descriptions convey the writer's strong feelings.

14 Logical connective associated with cause.

15 Logical connective associated with cause: all the preceding points lead up to the final result – a protest.

individuals[16] to organise a protest outside school on Friday. Miss Fussdom, there is an angry picket-line, ready to force you to back down!

Yours sincerely[17]

Letitia Hayworth

Flete House
Cushing Way
Stringley

To the Editor

Dear Sir[18]

I am in Year 9 of Free-For-All School, and have definite opinions of my own about wearing uniforms. The lack of a uniform encourages maturity, and helps people[19] to identify with their teachers as equals, and to behave in a more grown-up manner. It is one of the reasons why the young elect to go to Free-For-All, so[20] how can it be fair to introduce a uniform once I am at the school?

This right is long-existing, established a long time before this head came; as a result,[20] she cannot alter it. A change makes the school a different one, one that many refuse to accept!

Yours faithfully
Daisy Hopkins
Aged 14

---

91 Crispin Road
Grove Park Estate
Stringley

Dear Editor

(Please will you not print my name in the paper, as I am afraid of what other pupils at school can do.)

I have been reading the letters about Free-For-All in your paper, and I want people to know what I think. Not every pupil likes to wear her own choice of clothes to school. It is all right if you have lots of fashionable things, but otherwise[21] you keep getting teased and laughed at.

My parents are not well-off, and my mother is always saying that I need to wear everything until it's too small and it's worn out. I hate going to school and being laughed at, so I think that Miss Fussdom's idea is really good. Then everyone looks the same, so[22] no one is bullied.

(Name and address supplied)

Free-For-All School
Topping Drive
Stringley
Warks
AB1 4YZ

Dear Sir

May I add my opinion to the current debate over school uniform? I have taught at Free-For-All for 20 years, relishing the harmony between staff, pupils and parents. The lack of a uniform is a positive, contributory factor, allowing the children to be viewed and treated as adults.[23]

16 Generalised participant which extends the viewpoint.

17 Correct punctuation and form for a letter to a named recipient.

18 The correct punctuation and form for a letter beginning in this way is as shown.

19 This use of generalised participants is effective in widening the opinion.

20 Logical connective.

21 Logical connective of opposition.

22 Logical connective of cause. It makes the letter emotionally powerful, as it points out that all the arguments and evidence lead to this logical opinion.

23 This letter is different from the others, as it is a discussion text within itself. The first paragraph seems to favour not having a uniform; after that, the opinion alters.

Nevertheless,[24] times change. I now witness a gradual erosion, not just in standards of dress, but also in standards of mutual respect. People are no longer treated with courtesy; individuals are labelled unfashionable; and some talk of the school losing its former, high reputation.[25]

Most disturbing of all is the blatant disregard for any authority. These figures speak for themselves:

During 1997 – pupil exclusion from the school: 2 cases.

During 2002 – pupil exclusion from the school: 30 cases.[26]

Consequently,[27] there is urgent need for action, and I strongly welcome Miss Fussdom's proposals.

Yours faithfully

Susan Moorcroft

————————

Clearly, there are passionate and legitimate views on both sides of this argument. The concepts of freedom and maturity are important; but the concerns over a failure to respect authority and others' style of dress are also valid points.[28]

The debate continues. However, September is not very far away, and a decision is needed.[29]

24 Logical connective of opposition; its use is a good way to link one paragraph to the previous.

25 The list of evidence allows the writer to build up a strong 'case'.

26 Actual facts and figures often feature in discussion texts, as they are likely to be difficult to argue against.

27 This logical connective is used very appropriately, once all the proof for a need for action has been supplied.

28 A discussion text must supply a short summary of the main arguments on both sides.

29 The conclusion attempts to finish the text in a balanced way.

Understanding the grammar and punctuation

Grammar pointers

Connectives

These linking words or phrases play an important part in maintaining the cohesion of this text type. Logical connectives are the ones likely to feature in a discussion text. There are two types:

Cause

These help to draw arguments together. Emphasise to the children their value in reinforcing viewpoints. For example, the end of Susan Moorcroft's letter relies on her preceding evidence, and the logic of her viewpoint is emphasised with the use of a simple adverb, which acts as a connective:

> *Consequently, there is urgent need for action, and I strongly welcome Miss Fussdom's proposals.*

Another example is contained in the newsletter, where preceding evidence about standards of dress supports a logical conclusion:

> *Therefore, in September this year, a smart, grey and black school uniform will be introduced for every pupil.*

In the case of Daisy, she 'proves' she is right by saying that the rule cannot be changed because it was in place before the new head came. A connective phrase emphasises her logic:

> *This right is long-existing, established a long time before this head came; as a result, she cannot alter it.*

Opposition

Logical connectives may also focus on the other side of the argument. For example, the newspaper article attempts to give space to both sides, and to recognise the validity of both sets of opinions; the connectives used emphasise this. For example:

> *The concepts of freedom and maturity are important; but the concerns over a failure to respect authority and others' style of dress are also valid points.*

The reporter also sees room for a long debate, yet (this is a connective that shows opposition) points out that a decision is needed before the end of the school year:

> *The debate continues. However, September is not very far away, and a decision is needed.*

Punctuation pointers

Formal letters

Modern formal letters show considerable variety in their layout and punctuation. Examples within your school's correspondence might provide examples for discussion on the variation in punctuation. However, there are basic rules of punctuation to follow.

- The writer's address is divided into lines in the top right-hand corner of the letter. Commas and full stops are not required at the ends of the lines.
- Words such as 'road', 'drive' and 'way' normally begin with small letters; they begin with capital letters once they become part of a name:

> *Topping Drive*   *Cushing Way*

- The date, placed on a separate line under the writer's address, needs no punctuation.
- The address of the recipient of the letter is set out in lines on the left-hand side of the letter. Again, no punctuation is required.
- In modern convention, a comma is not usually used after the opening address. For example:

> *Dear Miss Fussdom*

- A new paragraph is begun immediately after this opening. For example:

> *Dear Sir*
>
> *I am in Year 9 of Free-For-All School, and...*

- Normal punctuation rules are adhered to for the body of the letter:

> *Our children maintain the right to be themselves, and, therefore, I am helping like-minded individuals to organise a protest outside school on Friday.*

- When the letter is signed off, no comma is needed:

> *Yours sincerely*
>
> *Letitia Hayworth*

The children's version of these notes is on page 93 of the resource book.

Writing features of discussion texts

Structure

- There must be a statement of the issue at the beginning of the text so that the topic under discussion is clear from the outset.

- The text needs to contain arguments from each side. In the exemplar, an equal balance is given by printing the same number of letters for and against. It would be interesting to discuss how fair this balance really is, because of the teacher's more articulate arguments and the emotionally-powerful anonymous letter .

- Presentation of viewpoints may vary:
  - one side at a time (ie all the arguments for, followed by all the arguments against);
  - both sides' arguments interwoven.

Ensure that the children recognise that the newspaper report represents one complete discussion text; the letters are part of it, as each only considers one side of the argument. The exception is Susan Moorcroft's letter, where points from both sides are considered:

> *The lack of a uniform is a positive, contributory factor, allowing the children to be viewed and treated as adults.*

(Here she acknowledges the benefits of not wearing a school uniform.)

> *Consequently, there is urgent need for action, and I strongly welcome Miss Fussdom's proposals.*

(Now she moves to the opposing camp.)

- Evidence is likely to feature in the text, as it is a strong way to argue a case. Miss Fussdom lists clothes that have upset her; Susan Moorcroft gives details of exclusion figures:

> *During 1997 – pupil exclusion from the school: 2 cases.*

> *During 2002 – pupil exclusion from the school: 30 cases.*

- The text needs a final summary of points from each side.

- Finally, the text finishes with a conclusion. In the exemplar, the danger of ongoing wrangling is recognised, as is the need of a decision in time for the new school year:

> *However, September is not very far away, and a decision is needed.*

Language

- The simple present tense is the correct tense for this text type. Point out to the children how much more passionate and urgent beliefs can sound when this tense is used. For example here:

> *and some talk of the school losing its ... reputation*

(This conveys urgency in a way that *have talked* would fail to do.)

> *Horrified, I hold a directive from you.*

(Again, a simple present tense is the most effective choice, conveying the greatest emotion.)

- References to non-specific participants (as opposed to individuals) make viewpoints wider and stronger. Words referring to generalised participants are a significant feature of this text type. The exemplar contains numerous examples:

> *I am helping like-minded individuals.*

(There is no way that Miss Fussdom can know from this phrase the size of the opposition she faces.)

> *It is ... why the young elect to go to Free-For-All.*

(Daisy's words give the impression that the choice of school is up to the children. It is a much more effective argument than simply saying 'I'.)

- If the opinions are strongly felt, the language used must show that. Stress to the children that words may have two roles:
  - they display the passion the writer feels;
  - they intend to cause a reaction.

For example, Mrs Hayworth uses words that show her anger and are meant to intimidate:

> *Horrified, I hold a directive from you, which demands...*

> *there is an angry picket-line, ready to force you to back down!*

- Remind the children of the usefulness of logical connectives. They maintain the cohesion of the text, making arguments appear more rational; they are also used to introduce opposing views. These words are likely to be particularly useful:

> *therefore*   *because*   *however*

There are helpful hints for children on writing a discussion text on page 96 of the resource book.

Editorials

A newspaper is a powerful medium, conveying information to a mass of people. Most of this information is fact rather than opinion, but the editorial is the section of the newspaper where a clear viewpoint is expressed. It is a piece of persuasive writing, looking at an issue of the moment, and putting forward a logical argument. In doing this, the editorial must appeal to its audience.

However, the newspaper must be aware of who its audience is, and it is for this reason that tabloid and broadsheet styles differ. The argument must be propounded in a style that will strike a chord, if it is to win agreement. Such persuasion is attempted in the vocabulary used and the references made: strong, emotive language is likely to stir up feelings, and alarming, emotive concepts to win support.

Having worked on the emotions, logic and reason must be evident. Effective support for the argument can come from various sources: facts and figures; reasons; and quotes from respected sources. The final summing-up emphasises the validity of the argument and reinforces the editorial's viewpoint.

Tabloids and broadsheets do have different styles. A tabloid's argument on an issue may sensationalise or exaggerate some factors, compared with the restrained tone and more reasoned and complex approach of the broadsheet. In this way, the writing reflects the reading patterns and tastes of the audiences. However, both papers retain the same aim: to persuade an audience of the validity of their arguments and to win that audience's agreement.

Editorials

Examples of editorials

Use editorials in different types of newspapers:

local
regional
national
tabloid
broadsheet

Useful references:

Newspaper Library
Colindale Avenue
London NW9 5HE
Tel: 0207 412 7353

For details of specific newspapers:
Writers' and Artists' Yearbook (A&C Black)

The children's version of the editorials is on page 105 of the resource book.

Newspaper editorials

THE PLANET SAYS[1]

CITY CENTRES FOR THE PEOPLE

IT'S ABOUT TIME WE GOT OUR ROADS BACK![2]

Does the car belong in town?[3] City centres are busy places, so[4] at least we need to feel safe there.

As[5] the number of cars increases, so[5] asthma figures are up 40%[6] on ten years ago.

[7]This must prove that the car is to blame. Cars just bring traffic fumes, congestion, air pollution, and maiming and life-wasting accidents.[8] If[5] cars only do harm, then[5] why not keep them away from these crowded areas?[9] We can try walking – walking kills no one – or even a cheap bus ride. It's better than risking death every time we go shopping.[10]

There are plenty of park-and-ride schemes, meaning that cars stay on the outskirts of town, and the centres obviously[11] stay car free. Of course,[11] keep a lane for buses and emergency vehicles, while[11] allowing the rest of the road to be pedestrianised – so that way there's **safe** room for everyone.[12]

Fred Chutney, the Equality Party's spokesman on transport, said this week: "There are 200 needless, appalling road accidents in city centres every day. Something must change."[13]

Chutney is right. Asthma, injuries and deaths tell us that shoppers and cars just do not mix.

Our government needs to ban cars NOW![14]

---

1 This is a typical tabloid title for its editorial page.

2 The heading and subheading immediately address the issue, and make the editorial's stance clear. The emotive language of the subheading gives the impression that people are being wronged. 'We' in the subheading puts editorial and audience on the same side, an effective, persuasive device.

3 The issue is introduced clearly at the outset.

4 A logical connective, linking the concepts of a busy place and the need to feel safe.

5 The two words work together to form a logical connective.

6 Statistical data are a strong support for an argument.

7 A logical connective is an effective link between the two paragraphs. A new paragraph has been begun to keep the ideas in manageable bites.

8 This sentence supplies further evidence of the damage cars do, giving more reasons for a ban.

9 A question directed to the audience is an effective device. Having persuaded the audience that an answer is needed, the text then supplies the answer.

10 This emotive concept, rather overstating the risk, is typical of a tabloid.

11 Logical connectives stress the value of the editorial's argument.

12 Emotive word that the editorial wants to be noticed is emphasised by highlighting.

13 A quote from a knowledgeable source supplies strong support.

14 A brief, final paragraph sums up the editorial's argument, picking up the 'we' used in line 2 and the subheading.

THE DAILY WINDOW[15]

CARS V PEOPLE
THE CAR NEEDS TO LOSE[15]

Our city centres are clogged with cars.[16] The number of cars has risen dramatically[17] over the last ten years, as our wealth has grown and our commuting requirements have become ever more urgent.[17]

The car may provide freedom of choice, but at what cost? It has become a threat to the nation's health,[18] in terms of a decline in our fitness.

Britain has the worst record in Western Europe for dangerous heart conditions; and a 40% rise in asthma cases;[19] and, of course,[20] the inevitable injuries and deaths. These are not the hallmarks of a civilized society.[21]

Logic says that if[22] these illnesses and accidents have risen to match our use of the car, then[22] the car must be the problem.

Consequently,[23] the problem needs to be addressed. Trial schemes in Manchester,[24] where clean, free park-and-ride buses ferry people between city centre and suburbs, are hailed as a resounding success, which proves that[25] public demand is there. Limited access to the city centre for only those buses, a controlled number of taxis and, of course,[25] emergency vehicles, allows for a considerable degree of pedestrianisation, which means that[25] people can walk further and in safety.[26]

Fred Chutney, the Equality Party's spokesman on transport, spoke out bravely[27] this week: "There are 200 needless, appalling road accidents in city centres every day. Something must change."[28]

As a result,[29] Parliament is currently debating this issue, but brave, expensive action is needed: in other words,[29] public transport must be improved.

Growing numbers of sick people, and shameful accident figures warn us that the car is no longer the way forward. **It must be removed from the city centre.**[30]

---

15 The broadsheet's title is straightforward and formal. The heading and subheading immediately address the issue, and make the editorial's stance clear, but the language is restrained.

16 The issue is introduced clearly at the outset.

17 Strong, emotive words. This statement is then supported by evidence about fitness, heart conditions and so on.

18 An emotive concept, likely to worry the audience.

19 Statistical data are a strong support for an argument.

20 Logical connective.

21 Notice the more sophisticated language of this broadsheet editorial, as well as the greater complexity of its language and message.

22 The two words work together to form a logical connective.

23 An effective choice of adverb, acting as a logical connective.

24 The Manchester scheme is used as evidence to support the argument.

25 Logical connectives.

26 An emotive concept, implicitly warning the audience of what will happen if this argument is not followed. (Notice again that the paragraph is longer and more complex than most of the tabloid's.)

27 An emotive word, emphasising the gravity of the situation.

28 A quote from a knowledgeable source supplies strong support.

29 Logical connectives.

30 A brief, final paragraph sums up the editorial's argument.

Understanding the grammar and punctuation

Grammar pointers

Using connectives

The linking words and phrases known as connectives are an important tool when writing an editorial. Logical connectives, dealing with cause and effect, are prevalent in editorials, aiding the construction of a persuasive argument.

Talk to the children about how the text needs to supply support for the argument, leading up to connectives such as *so* and *this shows that*, before supplying the logical conclusion. It is as if the argument has then been proved. For example:

> *City centres are busy places, <u>so</u> at least we need to feel safe there.*

(The two concepts of a busy place and personal safety are linked.)

A single word, such as *clearly* or *obviously*, can strengthen the apparent correctness of an argument, as well as phrases such as *of course*, and *meaning that*.

> *There are plenty of park-and-ride schemes, <u>meaning that</u> cars stay on the outskirts of town, and the centres <u>obviously</u> stay car free. <u>Of course,</u> keep a lane for buses and emergency vehicles, <u>while</u> allowing the rest of the road to be pedestrianised – <u>so</u> that way there's **safe** room for everyone.*

The editorial's argument may employ different types of connectives in its structure:

- Adverbs: *again; finally; consequently*

  > <u>*Consequently,*</u> *the problem needs to be addressed.*

- Adverbial phrases, or pairs of conjunctions (coordinating correlatives): on the other hand; if ... then

  > *Logic says that <u>if</u> these illnesses and accidents have risen to match our use of the car, <u>then</u> the car must be the problem.*

  (Notice that the two words work as a pair, creating a strong argument.)

- Conjunctions: *though, while*

  > <u>*while*</u> *allowing the rest of the road to be pedestrianised*

- Verb forms: *proving; which means...*

  > <u>*which proves*</u> *that public demand is there*

Emphasise that these connectives play a significant role in maintaining the cohesion of the text, and in producing a convincing, persuasive editorial.

Punctuation pointers

Speech marks

When quoting other people's exact words, inverted commas or quotation marks are required.

> *Fred Chutney, the Equality Party's spokesman on transport, said this week: "There are 200 needless, appalling road accidents in city centres every day. Something must change."*

Make sure that the children recognise that the exact words must be repeated for speech marks to be needed. (This is direct speech.)

If the message is merely reported, which means not quoting the exact words used, then quotation marks should not be used. (This is indirect speech.) For example, the text could say this:

> *Fred Chutney, the Equality Party's spokesman on transport, said this week that there are 200 needless, appalling road accidents in city centres every day. He stressed that something must change.*

This is reported speech, and no speech marks are used.

> The children's version of these notes is on page 106 of the resource book.

The writing features of editorials

An editorial – like any persuasive writing – needs to win over its audience. To do this, it must use the right words and the right arguments, as well as adopt a tone to suit that audience.

Structure

✦ The heading and subheading perform a number of functions. They:

- identify the issue (for example, 'Cars v People')
- show the editorial's stance on the issue ('The car needs to lose')
- appeal to the audience ('The car needs to lose')

✦ The issue needs to be introduced early on. There must be a clear opening statement or question doing this.

Does the car belong in town?

Our city centres are clogged with cars.

✦ The arguments put forward by an editorial need to be logical. They are likely to have support from:

1) Evidence

The number of cars has risen dramatically over the last ten years.

2) Statistics

As the number of cars increases, so asthma figures are up 40% on ten years ago.

3) Reasons

If cars only do harm, then why not keep them away from these crowded areas?

4) Quotes from people

Fred Chutney, the Equality Party's spokesman on transport, said this week: "There are 200 needless, appalling road accidents in city centres every day. Something must change."

✦ A summary of the arguments must conclude the editorial, accompanied by a final appeal to the audience. The broadsheet is likely to have offered a wider discussion than the tabloid, and therefore often has a longer, more complex summing-up:

*As a result, Parliament is currently debating this issue, but brave, expensive action is needed: in other words, public transport must be improved. Growing numbers of sick people, and shameful accident figures warn us that the car is no longer the way forward. **It must be removed from the city centre.***

In both styles, however short the editorial has been, this summary concludes with a final opinion:

It must be removed from the city centre.

Our government needs to ban cars NOW!

Language

✦ **Tense** – Newspaper editorials are current literature, so the **present tense** predominates.

✦ **Style** – The style must suit the audience. The newspaper knows its audience. Therefore, vocabulary, reading difficulty, complexity of ideas, and the tone adopted are all necessary considerations.

✦ **Logical connectives** – The arguments propounded must be convincing and, therefore, logical; the connectives used should emphasise this logic. The right connectives are able to persuade by making an argument appear obviously the right one. For example:

Consequently, the problem needs to be addressed. (With a single adverb, it now seems impossible to argue against what is being said.)

The following are all everyday examples of logical connectives:

proving that; therefore; as a result; of course; this shows; consequently; so; because; however

✦ **Emotive language** stirs up strong feelings, pulling the audience into the same mood as the editorial. Such language is seen, particularly, in tabloids.

We need to feel safe there. (Now the editorial and the audience are concerned together about safety.)

maiming and life-wasting accidents (A horrifying picture is painted.)

✦ **Emotive concepts** can have an even stronger effect, frightening the audience about future possibilities.

It's better than risking death every time we go shopping.

There are helpful hints for children on writing an editorial on page 109 of the resource book.